Plugging Into the Spirit of Prophecy

Adding Power to Your Prophetic Words

Scott Wallis

© 2001 by Scott Wallis

Plugging into the Spirit of Prophecy
by Scott Wallis

Printed in the United States of America
ISBN 1-931232-21-0

All rights reserved. No part of this publication may be reproduced or transmitted in any form or by any means without written permission of the publisher.

Unless otherwise indicated, Bible quotations are taken from the King James Version.

Xulon Press
11350 Random Hill Center
Suite 800
Fairfax, VA 22030
(703) 279-6511
XulonPress.com

Foreword

You are about to read a book that will awaken a renewed awareness of the presence of God in your life. Through this book, you will discover what God thinks about you. And as you are about to find out, His thoughts can be quite different from our own.

Since the Sept. 11th tragedy, we have all experienced a new call to freedom in this country. We have found out just how precious the gift of freedom we have is and why we must fight for it. Moreover, we have experienced firsthand the terror in the world.

During times like these, it is easy to become fearful. We can walk in a spirit of fear rather than the spirit of freedom that God designed us to walk in as believers. Because of this, we need to hear clearly what the Holy Spirit is saying to us. We need men and women of God who can help us hear God during these dark times with a clear word from heaven.

My son, Scott Wallis, has a clear word from heaven for you. After reading this book, you will move into a closer walk with Christ through God's Holy Spirit of prophecy. I feel blessed in writing this foreword for him. Not only because he is my son, but because of the man that I know him to be.

Scott grew up in a family that I imagine was much like yours. Our home was an average American home. Our neighborhood was an average American neigh-

• Plugging into the Spirit of Prophecy •

borhood. We experienced the ups and downs all families do. Our lives were filled with moments of love, joy, happiness and sadness.

There are many things about my son you will probably never know. I have seen him laugh and cry. I have seen him sitting on the sofa watching television. I have seen him wake up in the middle of the night with a bad dream. I have comforted and cared for him when he was sick. And I have seen just some of the trials that he has experienced, as well as the persistence he has walked in to get to this point.

From the moment my son was born, I knew he was blessed by God. As he grew older, this became more evident to me because he was never in trouble. When confronted by difficult choices, Scott always seemed to make the right decisions. I could always count on my son to do what was right. The one constant in my life was my son, Scott.

Over the years, I just laid all these things up in my heart. I never imagined that Scott would experience what he did in 1987 when he was called by God. At first I didn't fully understand the transformation that was taking place in my son. Yet the peace I saw in him was undeniable, and it caused me to start seeking the Lord for myself.

Unbeknownst to Scott, I began reading the Bible,

• Foreword •

searching for answers to the dramatic changes I saw in him. I saw that what he had was real, and this led me into my own personal experience with God. I began feeling the Lord in my life as I had never felt Him before.

It was through this searching that I began to understand that Scott was on a journey toward something that he saw, but that I didn't fully understand. Even as I am writing the foreword for this book, I don't claim to understand fully what my son is saying. What I do know is that after I read my son's first book on prophecy, *How to Know if Your Prophecy Is Really From God*, I started understanding it was God's will for my son to bring the power of the prophetic word to people through his ministry.

As you begin your journey into this book about plugging into the Spirit of prophecy with my son, Scott, you will gain a deeper understanding of God and the way He speaks to us through prophecy. My prayer is that if you open your heart, as I have, you, too, will hear God's words and learn from Him as He speaks to us through His spokesmen and spokeswomen—His prophets.

—Joan Wallis

Contents

Foreword v
Introduction xiii
Chapter One
    The Nature of Prophecy 1
Chapter Two
    The Work of Prophecy..23
Chapter Three
    The Word of Prophecy 45
Chapter Four
    The Hearing Ear and Seeing Eye 61
Chapter Five
    As Dew in the Morning...77
Chapter Six
    Flowing in the Holy Spirit 97
A Final Word..113

Introduction

"Follow after charity, and desire spiritual gifts, but rather that ye may prophesy."
1 Cor. 14:1

The apostle Paul defines prophecy as a gift from God to believers for the edification of the church. The Spirit of Prophecy, or the Holy Spirit, is the giver of this gift. To refuse the gift of prophecy is to refuse the Holy Spirit Himself.

The scripture speaks of the gift of prophecy when it instructs us to "quench not the Spirit" (1 Thes. 5:19). Therefore, when the gift of prophecy is quenched, so is the Spirit of prophecy, which is the vehicle God uses to communicate the gospel of His Son to lost humanity (Rev. 19:10).

Quench Not the Spirit

Far too many of those involved in world evangelism quench the spirit behind evangelism, the Spirit of prophecy, and refuse to hear or allow Him to speak in their midst. The gift of prophecy is quenched, the office of prophet is denounced, and the Spirit of prophecy is grieved. In essence, they have closed the door to the person who is most willing to help them accomplish the great task of world evangelization.

How sad! No wonder we have fallen so far short in our attempts to reach the world for Jesus Christ—we have sought to do it in our own strength. We need to repent for hurting and grieving the Holy Spirit by denying His voice and quenching His flow (Acts 3:19). Unless we do this first, we will not see the work of evangelism completed in our generation, but will have shifted our responsibility to yet another generation, delaying the coming of Christ once again.

I can only imagine what Jesus must think. The epitome of patience, he has been waiting for nearly 2000 years to receive His bride, painfully hindered by His own leaders. We have stood in His way rather than standing by His side. Oh, that we would lay down our ways and thoughts and pick up God's thoughts through the Spirit of prophecy (Is. 55:9).

• Introduction •

Living in a New Day—a New Way

Please hear me: we are at the verge of a moment like no other. The Holy Spirit is seeking to spark within the church a holy passion for the Savior through the vehicle of prophecy once again. The prophetic ministry is about to experience a huge increase, and the Spirit of prophecy will bless those who support it. They will find their destiny in Christ as the Spirit of prophecy is released into their lives. This is something we desperately need in our day. Praise God!

We need the voice of prophecy, for it enables the church to mature in Christ. God has chosen this divine vehicle to speak to His people and help them realize who they are in Him and who He is in them. Prophecy should reveal to us the mysteries of Christ, the wonders of God, and the thoughts of God toward us, both individually and corporately (1 Cor. 13:2).

Can you imagine what it would be like to know exactly what God thinks about you? Prophecy is designed to reveal His thoughts toward us. If we could catch a glimpse of what God really thinks about us, our lives would be revolutionized. We would be so captured by the love of our Savior that we would not fear the enemy who is fighting so hard against us. We would be willing to endure anything to see Him.

The early disciples were certain of what God was saying to them every day, which radically changed them and their culture. Because they heard clearly what God was saying and were willing to die for Him, tension existed between believers and unbelievers in the early church. They did not fear death because Christ was exalted in their minds through the Spirit of prophecy.

Genuine Prophecy—What We Crave

We need this! The enemy has fought hard against prophecy in the church, attempting to prevent us from reaching full stature in Christ. The enemy knows that his time is short (1 Cor. 7:29, Mt. 8:29). He is seeking to delay his predetermined prison sentence from the Judge of the Universe, God Himself. To do this, he has sought to silence the voice of prophecy in the church, preventing the maturity of Christ's church for His coming.

Do you see the importance of prophecy to the church? It is vital for us to understand what prophecy is and how it works, and to know God and why He has given it. In this book I am seeking to cover areas of prophecy where other authors have been silent. My desire is to help the church mature in prophetic ministry so that she can hear what the Holy Spirit—the Spirit of prophecy—is speaking to her.

Because this topic is somewhat unusual, I ask you to search the scriptures to ascertain the truth of what I am saying (Acts 17:11). I believe that the ultimate voice of prophecy in the church is the Holy Bible (2 Pet. 19). Whenever we open this holy book, we should hear from God (2 Tim. 3:16). I write to share what I have learned through the eyes of experience and the lens of the scriptures.

The Greatest Mind on Earth

The Bible says, "we know in part, and we prophesy in part" (1 Cor. 13:9). This means that no individual has a complete picture of what God is doing on earth. We need to learn from one another what God is speaking to each of us. When we hear what God is speaking, we start to partake of the mind of Christ, which is resident in the church (1 Cor. 2:16). The church has within her the treasures and mysteries of Christ (2 Cor. 4:7). This is an awesome realization.

You are part of the great mind of Christ, which is resident in you through the community of the church. When we gather together, we are to hear from God and be channels through which God can speak. This is what Peter meant when he said, "if any man speak, let him speak as the oracles of God" (1 Pet. 4:11). We are called to be holy oracles speaking the mysteries of God to those who come before us.

The greatest pool of revelation and wisdom in the earth today is largely untapped because the church has closed her ears to the Spirit of prophecy in her midst. We have allowed the enemy to pull people into his kingdom because we have neglected to hear and speak the voice of God. Psychics, mediums, and soothsayers have prospered because the church has remained silent. We need to repent and begin honoring God's Spirit of prophecy in our midst once again.

Listen to a Voice of Reason

Will you lay aside your contentions for just a moment? Will you look beyond your own emotional well-being and satisfaction? Will you begin to search the scriptures with me to see what it says about prophecy? I am asking you to lay aside your preconceived notions and to hear what I have to say about this very important subject. You may hear some things with which you will disagree. Are you willing to do this?

I trust that you will listen to the voices of reason, scripture, and prophecy as we move forward. This book is designed to challenge some of the teachings prevalent in the church today. I am not doing this to create controversy, even though I know controversy is inevitable. My desire in this is not only to expose some un-Biblical teachings, but also to help the church discover what the scriptures have to say about prophecy.

So with ears intently open, let us begin our journey into understanding the nature of prophecy. As we do this, we will look at what prophecy is and what it is not. We will see what its function is in the church and what it is not. We will find the guidelines in the scriptures about flowing in the Spirit of prophecy and yielding to His voice. As we do this, we will learn more about God's great gift of prophecy and the giver, which is the Spirit of prophecy.

Knowing What We Have in Christ

Prophecy is one of the most overlooked gifts in the church today. Even though many people claim to function in this gift, few have realized its awesome importance and the breadth of its scope. To truly have the gift of prophecy functioning in the church would awaken us to things that the human mind has not even conceived. We would open a world of mystery still yet uncharted and too vast for comprehension.

We need some spiritual pioneers who are willing to go the extra mile to chart the mysteries of God lying hidden, awaiting discovery by the Spirit of prophecy. What wonders we would behold if we would just listen to the Spirit of prophecy, beckoning to us to come hither. The universe itself would be an open book to us. The heavens would be rolled back and the mysteries of life revealed. Things stored up for ages and generations would be made known to the church (Eph. 3:5). We would see His glory.

All of creation speaks to testify of the hidden glories of God (Ps. 19:1). Nature itself reveals a portion of His mysteries awaiting discovery. We are surrounded by untapped and unused resources. Everything that we know is but a shadow of what is to be discovered.

This is an awesome reality that the church has yet to grasp. We are journeying toward a new frontier of understanding, and the only map available is hidden in the church.

The church contains more than she has realized. We have the keys that will unlock the gates of heaven and overcome the gates of hell (Mt. 16:18,19). This is power. How do you think this will happen? Do you think that one day we are suddenly going to be overwhelmed by indescribable power and bind the devil? The only way this will happen is if we learn to hear what the Spirit of prophecy is saying in our midst.

The Rock of Revelation

This is the rock that Jesus will use to build His church. When we stand upon this foundation, the church will grow. When we start moving in revelation and understanding about the mysteries of God, the devil will be bound and the bride of Christ loosed. We will be loosed upon a world that has been ravaged and raped by the enemy of souls. There will be so many ministry needs that we will have to let Christ do the work through us. May God bring us to this point.

This is the effect that prophecy can have on the church and the world. Prophecy is a beacon that summons us to something that is yet unseen. In other words, prophecy brings us to the point of faith. We will believe to see the goodness of the Lord in the land of the living (Ps. 27:13). Prophecy will bring us into a wide and spacious place. We will have the vision necessary to avoid the snares and traps that Satan has set for us. We will overcome the evil one with the good of prophecy. This is the sword of the Spirit (Eph. 6:17).

The sword of the Spirit is the prophetic word. When we hear the Spirit of prophecy, we are allowing God to place a sword in our hands to use in combat against the evil forces that hold this world in bondage. Fear will depart, faith will rise, and God will be glorified. The enemy of our souls will be bound and captives will be set free. True liberty will enter the church as she hears the voice of prophecy in her midst. We will be liberated from the devil's strongholds that have held us in bondage.

A Voice Can Shake the World

Think for a moment about the effect Martin Luther King had upon a whole society. His voice still echoes through time today, calling men and women everywhere to be free from the chains of racism. Many have tried to imitate him and have fallen short. Why is this? Because they have not heard the prophetic voice of the Spirit as clearly as Martin Luther King did, even though they may have a strong desire to see racism end. He was a prophet ahead of his time who saw the mystery of God concerning the end of racism.

• Plugging into the Spirit of Prophecy •

We need the voice of prophecy in our midst today. We need the Spirit of prophecy to inspire us. We need holy men and women of God who are moved upon and carried by the Holy Spirit as He wills (2 Pet. 2:21). We need power from on high (Acts 1:8). We need a fresh baptism of the Holy Spirit, especially in the area of prophecy. We need God Himself to move upon us and liberate our tongues from the words of this world so that His words might be fitted within our mouths.

The old hymn proclaims, "O for a thousand tongues to sing my great Redeemer's praise, the glories of my God and King, the triumphs of His grace!" Just musing on this song causes me to wonder how far we have fallen away from the Spirit of revelation and prophecy in the church. I don't know about you, but I am convicted by these lyrics. Why? Because they have something that so few of our songs do today—they have heart. God's truth is in them, and this we lack.

Getting Back to Basics

I do not mean to condemn the Christian music industry today. I am merely making an observation about how rich the old hymns are in the Holy Spirit's presence. The truth is, the authors of these hymns heard and communicated something deeper than the words they wrote—they heard the voice of God through the Spirit of prophecy.

This is why so much power resides in the old hymns today. After all these years, the Spirit of prophecy who birthed these hymns still resides in them. Can we say the same thing about our lives and music? Or do we fall short of what our predecessors have done?

I think that one reason we have so little power in the church today is we don't spend quality time with God individually. We have a microwave mentality about everything that God does. And in some cases, God has catered to our flesh. The truth is that we are not willing to wait for God's best, so we settle for something that is obviously less.

My hope in writing this book is to stir you up to seek something from God that is better than what you already have, especially in the area of prophecy. Something better awaits the church in prophecy. God desires to satiate our thirst in this area. We can have more, God wants us to have more, and nothing can stop us except us. As someone has once said, "We have seen the enemy, and the enemy is us."

Let's Go Higher

We are our own worst enemy. You are the only one who can stop you from moving in the Spirit of prophecy today. The grace of God is poured out upon the church for every member of the body to function in this realm. We have been given the grace and the anointing necessary to function more deeply in prophecy than many of us have dreamed. What we call the prophetic today has barely touched the river of prophecy that flows from God's throne. Open your heart and life to something more.

My desire as we move forward in this book is to communicate that more is available to us. There is a deeper, richer, purer realm of prophecy available to the church. As such, through the Spirit of prophecy I am calling you to "come ye, and let us go up to the mountain of the Lord, to the house of the God of Jacob; and He will teach us of His ways, and we will walk in His paths: for out of Zion shall go forth the law, and the word of the Lord from Jerusalem" (Is. 2:3). Amen.

Chapter One

The Nature of Prophecy

"Again He said unto me, Prophesy upon these bones, and say unto them, O ye dry bones, hear the word of the Lord. Thus saith the Lord God unto these bones; Behold, I will cause breath to enter into you, and ye shall live."

Ezekiel 37:4,5

Do you hear the call to prophecy that is reverberating throughout the church? God is calling His people to move into the realm of prophecy. We are to be a prophetic people, and the church a prophetic church. The Spirit of prophecy is to be moving fluidly in our midst. Nothing should hinder the prophetic flow in our lives or in the church, and yet many things do. Why? Because we really have not understood the nature of prophecy.

I believe that much of the teaching available today on the prophetic ministry has brought confusion. Instead of having a clear stream of prophecy flowing from God's throne, we have muddied it up through our own impure motives (Ezek. 34:18). We have prophesied out of our gift rather than out of God's heart; consequently, few people have really been touched or transformed by the prophetic word. We have given out words that are ineffective.

Changing the Prophetic Climate in the Church

Is prophecy supposed to be ineffective? How can we claim to be prophesying by the Spirit and yet see so few lives changed by the prophetic word? This calls into question the voice with which we are speaking. We are giving an unclear sound, and the body of Christ is largely confused about what prophecy is and what it can do (1 Cor. 14:8). We do not know what to believe or who to believe, and for the most part we have excluded everyday people from prophesying, leaving it to the masters of the prophetic realm.

Yet our prophetic gurus are in many ways filled with guile and deceitfulness. They have chosen to administer prophecy in the world's way through the world's means. As such, the prophetic movement has largely strayed from the Spirit of prophecy that birthed it and entered into the spirit of Balaam (2 Pet. 2:15). Greed has replaced God as the motivation behind giving the prophetic word. We have sold doves in God's house and Jesus is upset about this (John 2:16). It is time for a change.

The prophetic community and the church must live above reproach if we are to rise above the voice of skepticism and criticism that seeks to drown out our voice. <u>Accuracy is not the primary measurement for whether a prophecy is true. We can give an accurate word and that word can be completely false—it may have even come from a demonic source.</u> Listen to me: we need to change the measurement by which we judge our prophecies and the prophecies of others.

For this to happen, we need to base our practices on the word of God. We must rediscover what the Bible, especially the New Testament, teaches about judging prophecy. Once we have laid a good foundation for what the New Testament says about prophecy, then we can move to what the Old Testament says.

Becoming Fluent in the Language of Prophecy

Why am I starting with the New Testament version of prophecy? Because we need to understand that prophecy, although the same gift in both the Old and New Testaments, has served different roles in different time periods. The role of prophecy in the New Testament is far different from the Old Testament. This means that it is judged by different standards. As such, we need to identify the New Testament standards for judging prophecy.

This brings us to the place in scripture with the clearest instruction about New Testament prophecy: 1 Corinthians 12–14. Within these chapters, Paul gives clear instruction about prophecy, including what it is and how it is to be handled. In other words, prophecy needs to be handled with care, for it is explosively powerful when used properly. We can even come to the place where the church is so fluent in this gift that an unbeliever would come into the church and be converted through its influence (1 Cor. 14:24,25).

Wouldn't you like the church to come to this place in our ability to prophesy? We can! It is God's design. He wants us to prophesy more than we want to do it. Why? Because when prophecy is flowing smoothly in the church, it brings us into a whole new dimension of spirituality—a place called the sovereign will of God.

This is why Paul encourages believers at Corinth to covet this precious gift (1 Cor. 12:31, 14:1). We are to literally have a lust in our hearts to prophesy.

These are strong words. Remember these are not the words of a man but of God. Why would God want us to have a lust to prophesy? Because our tongues, when used rightly, can bring blessing. The primary area where most believers have problems is with the tongue. According to James, "The tongue is a fire a world of iniquity…" (James 3:6). The tongue can create more havoc in a moment than any other member of the body could do in a lifetime.

Prophecy Can Tame Your Tongue

Maybe this is why Peter said, "If any man speak, let him speak as the oracles of God…" (1 Pet. 4:11). These are strong words in defense of prophecy. Paul, Peter, and James all encourage us to replace our own words with the words of God. There must be something to prophecy that is far more important than we have ever realized in the church. And if we could ever catch a glimpse of what our words can do in the lives of those around us, it would forever change the way we speak—we wouldn't want to do anything but prophesy.

Moses, one of the greatest prophets to ever walk the face of this earth, said, "Would God that all the Lord's people were prophets, and that the Lord would put His Spirit upon them!" (Num. 11:29.) Why would

Moses say this? Because Moses understood the danger of the tongue. He had firsthand experience in dealing with people who had uncircumcised lips. The tongue of the Israelites did more damage to them than Egypt, their worst enemy. More people were destroyed by the wayward tongue and what came out of it than by all of Pharaoh's armies (1 Cor. 10:10).

Think about this for a moment. More believers are destroyed by their own tongues than the devil is able to kill in a thousand years. No wonder James encourages us to keep our tongues in check. I think if we said less, did more, and prayed more, we would have far fewer problems as believers in this world. In fact, I believe the tongue is the primary source of the problems we face in this life. We need a change of mouth and a change of heart.

Giving Your Tongue to God

Many believers are comfortable with allowing God to change their hearts. They will say, "Lord, have your way in my heart." The problem comes when He wants to have His way with our tongues. No wonder we are so adamant in our disputes over the reality of prophecy—we don't want to be held to a higher standard of accountability. The truth is, many of us are comfortable with our tongues because we are comfortable with our sins. We like our sin and don't want to give it up.

We like gossiping, slandering, accusing, criticizing, railing, nagging, and so on. We love these sins, for they give expression to what is in our hearts (Matt. 15:11). We don't want to give them up; we will say, "It is my right to say what I want." This is what embroils much of the body of Christ today. Sad to say, many ministers are as guilty of this as the rest of us (James 3:1,2). I think the sins of the tongue are more manifest in ministry than in any other place.

Forgive me for being blunt, but the truth needs to be told. We cannot lie to ourselves or to the Holy Spirit anymore. Our tongues are killing us. The church is divided because we have not learned how to control what we say (James 4:1). In the morning we say to our brothers and sisters in church "I love you," and then in the evening we will gossip over the phone about them. We call ourselves God's holy huddle or the prayer ministry or some other title to satisfy our scourged consciences.

Getting into the Spirit

We need to learn to prophesy so we will get out of the flesh and into the spirit (Gal. 5:16). Nothing is better for our spiritual lives than the ability to speak prophetically. We are cleansed as we prophesy or speak in tongues (Eph. 5:26). Our tongue is given over to God. This is good, holy, and right in His sight, which is why He desires that we covet to prophesy.

I believe that if we take this command of God seriously, we will see a greater demonstration of the Spirit of prophecy in our midst. We would come to the place where all prophesy as the scriptures teach us (1 Cor. 14:31). This is the heart of God and the desire of the Holy Spirit in our midst. The Triune God wants to be our God and to have His way in our services. Then we will receive the full blessing of the prophetic ministry.

Thank God for His mercy and patience toward us (Ex. 34:6,7). He is our greatest need, and when we receive prophetic ministry, this need is truly met. God uses prophecy to touch us in a way that no other ministry can. Even the highly treasured gift of healing pales in comparison to prophecy, for it can energize our spirit unlike any other gift. Prophecy fuels us to fulfill our destiny in Christ.

Plugging into the Power

Prophecy is a heavenly power source like no other. When we receive prophetic ministry, it can charge and enable us to do what would have been previously impossible. Prophecy imparts the power through the Holy Spirit to help us fulfill God's will for our lives. We need prophecy because it helps us do the will of the Father.

Do you want to do the will of your Father in heaven? If so, you will need to receive prophetic ministry. No matter how spiritual you might be, you cannot go without prophetic ministry and still fulfill God's ultimate will for your life. This may be hard to hear, but it is the truth, for the scriptures say, "Surely, God will do nothing but He revealeth His secret unto His servants the prophets" (Amos 3:7).

God has chosen to work through the vehicle of prophecy. No wonder the work of God has been so hindered in our day—we have chosen to despise this precious gift of God. If we would change our attitude toward this gift, then its administration would change our lives. We would open up a whole new world of forgotten possibility. The world of the impossible would become reality. Miracles would be manifested in our midst and the work of God would prosper through our lives daily. We would truly be rich.

Doing What God Says

But as it stands now, we are blind, wretched, poor, miserable, and naked, and yet we think we are rich (Rev. 3:17). We have deceived ourselves into believing a lie supported by our own limited perception of what we think God can do. The truth is that we have rarely seen the Spirit of God work in our lives because we have silenced His prophetic voice. How long will God allow this to go on?

The time will come when God will say enough is enough. The Lord says, "…My Spirit shall not always strive with man..." (Gen. 6:3). How long has the Spirit of prophecy been striving with us? How long have we closed our ears to His voice? When did we last hear what the Spirit is saying to the church? It is time for us to get real with God and with one another. We must lay aside the petty differences that have divided us and that have separated us from the real Spirit of prophecy.

Those who desire to hear and act must separate themselves from those who hear but choose to disobey and from those who are unwilling to hear at all. God will not allow our shallow, lukewarm lives to run rampant in His church forever. The entertainment style of Christianity that has supported sloppy spirituality is about to experience a rude awakening (Amos 4:12). God is in the house, and He is going to have His own way whether we like it or not. Or else!

Getting on God's Good Side

Or else what? Believe me, some things we just don't want to know, and this is one of them. We don't want to find ourselves fighting against God. Rather, we must choose to be on God's side, and to do whatever it takes to be there. We may experience short-term pain, but the rewards are eternal. I have chosen this investment that gains interest for all eternity. How about you?

The Spirit of God is calling the church to make a

choice, saying, "Choose you this day whom you will serve" (Josh. 24:15). The church is standing at a crossroads today: either we will allow the Holy Spirit the freedom of expression in our midst, or we will forfeit the lampstand that Christ has given to us (Rev. 2:5). It is that simple. The choice we make will have eternal consequences for the future of the church in this nation and world.

Prophecy Can Change Our Lives

This is the nature of prophecy: it is to challenge and to change us. When we receive prophetic words, God is telling us that we need to change. The more prophecy we receive, the more change we need. Those who receive abundant prophecy need to change abundantly. This is true whether the prophetic word is given for edification, exhortation, comfort, correction, direction, reproof, or rebuke. All of these prophetic words will bring change into our lives.

How does this change come? It comes through the vehicle of the prophetic word, which is more than just information or even revelation—it is a dynamic source of power for God's will in our lives. When prophecy is given, power is released for God's will to be done. He imparts something that wasn't in our lives prior to the prophecy.

This is why Paul charged Timothy, his son in the faith, saying, "This charge I commit unto thee, son

Timothy, according to the prophecies which went before on thee, that thou by them mightest war a good warfare" (1 Tim. 1:18). And again, "Neglect not the gift that is in thee, which was given thee by prophecy, with the laying on of the hands of the presbytery" (1 Tim. 4:14). Paul gave Timothy these commands to help him understand the importance of the prophecies he had received. They weren't just vain words, but they were working mightily in him to will and to do of God's good pleasure (Phil. 2:13).

So then, prophecy is more than just a mere recitation of facts or revelation of truth—it is an impartation of power. The prophetic word is designed to impart the power of the Holy Spirit so that we might do God's will. Maybe this is why Peter said on the day of Pentecost, "And your sons and daughters will prophesy" (Acts 2:17). By the outpouring of the Holy Spirit on that day, the conduit of His power—prophecy—had been opened.

What If God Really Had His Way?

Imagine what would happen if our sons and daughters prophesied like Peter predicted. Do you think they would be bored with church? Wouldn't it be one of the most exciting places on earth? Young people would flock to the church, yearning for Sovereign guidance and direction for their lives, finding their purpose and calling. This is the effect that genuine prophecy can have upon the hearts of generations to come—it can radically change them to the glory of God.

Don't our fleshly methods pale in comparison to the awesome ways of God? No wonder the scripture says, "the flesh profiteth nothing" (John 6:63). Maybe the church has seen little movement for so long because we have tried to function in the arm of our flesh rather than in the strength of the Spirit. Oh, that we would lay aside the distractions from the reality of God and choose the things that lead us into the deeper life of the Holy Spirit.

I believe it is time for us to arise out of the ashes of what we have built. We must begin seeking the face of God for the reality that proceeds out of His Spirit. We need the holy prophetic word to be spoken in the church once again, and we must seek the Lord until He comes (Hos. 10:12). We must pray until we penetrate the heavens and receive the anointed word of God. In this day we need a real word that will work real change for the glory of God in our midst.

This is what we need in our day—real answers from a real God doing a real work in our day. The time has come for us to leave our lukewarm state. Be filled with the fire of God and a holy passion from the heart of God. Be filled with the anointing of the Spirit of Prophecy that will break off every yoke from your life. Receive the engrafted prophetic word that will save your soul from a multitude of troubles and trials. Be revived by the Spirit and word of the Lord.

A Carrier of His Glory

God's power is manifested in prophecy. A charge of anointing comes when we receive prophecy, and our lives become energized with the Spirit of God. Prophecy, by nature, can do more in a moment that we can in a lifetime. One word from God can change everything, including your circumstances, your family, your marriage, your career path, and your housing. Most importantly, your destiny will change.

The prophetic word can change all these things and more. It can open what no man can shut, and shut what no man can open (Rev. 3:7). The anointed prophetic word can cause the waves of the sea to stand in a heap or can change water into wine. It is where miracles are born and God's gifts are given. This is why we need anointed prophecy in the church—we need miracles and gifts. We need the glory of God.

When the prophetic word comes, the glory of God is not far behind. Every prophetic word carries within it a measure of His glory. It is a channel for God to communicate His glory to us. The problem is that we have been tuning into the wrong station for far too long. We have bought the lies of the world and believed the lies of the devil. This is what has prevented us from receiving the prophetic word and an increase of God's glory in our midst.

Becoming Like Christ

Not only will the prophetic word bring change, power, and glory into our lives—it will also birth the nature of Jesus inside of us. The ultimate goal of prophecy is to prepare us to become more like Christ. The prophetic word reveals to us who we can be and who God designed us to be in Him. We see things from God's perspective rather than our own. God opens our eyes to behold Him, the author and finisher of our lives (Heb. 12:2).

God made you to be like Jesus. You were born to walk in the nature of Christ. Every person on Earth who comes to Christ will be gathered into Him so that He may be all in all (Eph. 1:10). This is God's ultimate purpose and plan for everyone. And everything that happens is preparing us for that day. We are being conformed into the image of Christ so that we will fit into place when that day comes.

Prophecy prepares the way for that day (Is. 40:3). The prophetic word is preparing the church to receive who God made her to be. It should open our eyes to what we have not seen, to what we have not heard, and to what we have not perceived. It should open to us new dimensions in our walk with God. Prophecy is designed to propel us to a place where we could not have gone ourselves.

Seeing What is Unseen

Somewhere along the line, the church received the wrong message about prophecy. She was taught that it only confirms what we ourselves have heard. Nothing could be further from the truth. It should open us up to receive more than we ever imagined. It should reveal new horizons of possibility beyond our expectations. Whole new arenas of thought should come through the vehicle of prophecy.

Are you ready? Do you want to receive? Will you lay aside your preconceived notions of what God will and won't do? God is more than willing to give us insight into things to come (John 16:13). The future is an open book to His mind. He doesn't separate the past from the present or the future when He looks into our lives. He sees who we will be, who we have been, and who we are right now. God knows the end from the beginning, and He wants to help us get to the finish line through the prophetic word.

Far too many Christians never reach their full potential. They are held back from becoming who God made them to be. And rather than get up and fight, they lie down and die (2 Kin. 7:3). The church has played dead for so long that we think we are dead when in reality we have only been afraid of our own shadow. It's time to stop boxing with the shadows that have held you back. The prophetic word can help you do this.

Our God Still Does Miracles

Ezekiel had a vision of a forgotten valley filled with dry bones (Ezek. 37). No one was around for miles except Ezekiel and God. God took Ezekiel through this valley where he could inspect the bones, and Ezekiel noticed that they were very dry. The bones had been lost for so long that the heavens themselves did not know of their existence, but God knew. And He was ready to do something about it.

God then asked Ezekiel, "Can these bones live?" What an absurd question. Didn't God know that the bones were already dead? The bones had no hope for life to be restored to them in the natural world. They were dead, dry bones, and yet God asked if they could live. This is the way God thinks. He sees what we would never even consider. He sees through the eyes of faith and possibility.

I love Ezekiel's response to God's question. He recognized that he didn't have the answer. From Ezekiel's vantage point (and ours), the bones were already dead and dry. But Ezekiel had enough sense to lay aside any preconceived notions and admit that he didn't know, but God did. I love this. God knows what He is doing. It is time for the church to truly believe that God knows what He is doing. We must ask for His help in discovering what He is doing so that we can be a part of it.

God Knows What He is Doing

God knows what He is doing. What a revelation! Oh, that the church would hear this message being communicated from the throne of God. He is able to raise up those He chooses, in His time, and in His way. I love David's words when he referred to Jesus being raised up as the Messiah. He said, "This is the Lord's doing; it is marvelous in our eyes" (Ps. 118:23). God knows what He is doing.

When Ezekiel admitted that God knew the answer, He was greatly pleased. Then the Lord opened Ezekiel's eyes and told him to prophesy. God didn't tell Ezekiel what to say, but God did tell Ezekiel that He would speak through him. So Ezekiel opened his mouth and prophesied that the bones would live, speaking life into them. He knew that God would do something bigger than he ever imagined as he commanded the bones to live.

Suddenly Ezekiel heard a sound. It began small, and then grew exceedingly loud. Bone joined to bone, and flesh covered them. God began working a miracle among those dead, dry bones. Everything was shaking; bones were flying everywhere; pandemonium, confusion, and disorder ruled the day. It seemed out of character for God to work this way. Doesn't He do things decently and in order? But His ways aren't always our ways, and neither are His thoughts our thoughts (Is. 55:8).

God knows what He is doing. When God speaks and things begin to happen, just know that God knows what He is doing. When things happen that seem to be out of control, just know that God knows what He is doing. When bones or people start flying all over the place, just know that God knows what He is doing. When people start to scream and holler, shout and pout over the confusion, and they say that you are out of order, just know that God knows what He is doing.

Making Prophecy Work for Us

This is the reality of prophecy: it doesn't always happen in a nice, neat, or sweet way. It can bring confusion, as when Ezekiel prophesied to the dry bones. Everything appeared out of order, and confusion reigned for a moment. But in the end, God had His way. The bones came together and became an exceedingly great army (Ezek. 37:10). Don't we want the church to become a great army of people who are ready to do battle with the enemy on his own turf?

Then we must allow the prophetic word to do its work. The problem is that we don't give the word the freedom necessary to grow in our lives, so it becomes short-circuited. As a result, the prophecy stagnates and becomes ineffective. The word is nullified by our inaction. Because of this, we lose what we were meant to receive—the blessing of God.

I don't know of any authors who have written about the work of prophecy. The reason we in the church are unwilling to support prophets is that we don't consider their calling to be work (1 Tim. 5:18). Few view prayer as work, and fewer still see prophecy this way. Most of the time we assume that these things come naturally. But they don't—it requires a great deal of preparation to deliver accurate, life-changing prophetic words hour after hour. This indeed is work.

Why am I bringing this up? Because unless we realize that prophecy is work, we will never understand that prophecy also does work. To help bring understanding in the work of prophecy, I will describe it in great detail in the next chapter. The work of prophecy brings great rewards. In truth, prophecy helps us to work smarter, not harder. We get more done with better results in less time, making our job in the church much easier.

Chapter Two

The Work of Prophecy

"For it is God which worketh in you both to will and do of His good pleasure."
Phil. 2:15

Prophecy is work and it does work in the church. This may sound like an amazing statement to you, but it is the truth. I have been a prophet for nearly 10 years, prophesying to thousands of individuals, including ministers, business people, and homemakers. Some of the things I told these individuals have proven invaluable in their ability to live fruitful lives. The prophecies have made it easier for them to live for the Lord.

I remember a couple that I prophesied to about having children with the following word: "The Lord says He makes the barren woman to rejoice and be the joyful mother of children." Soon after I spoke this word, the couple was able to adopt two lovely children. God answered the cry of their heart. Isn't God good!

I also remember prophesying to a businessman of a well-known chain. I spoke to this man when he was in the midst of a difficult situation that could have turned into a messy legal battle. The Lord spoke to him the following words through me: "…I will turn this situation around for you." In reality, the Lord spoke more than this to me. He gave me exact ages where He had helped this man previously. God was reminding this man of His blessings upon his life.

The prophetic words were instrumental in the lives of these individuals. Countless others have also received similar prophetic words. As I prophesied over these people, major changes for good have taken place in their lives. They were blessed by the prophetic word as it worked and bore fruit in their lives (Col. 1:6). The only problem is that few of these individuals have taken the time to bless me in my areas of need, or to even say "thank you," for that matter (Lk. 17:17).

This is how I came to realize that most people consider prophecy to be easy and to come naturally. They do not understand the amount of time, effort, and energy I must spend to keep myself spiritually fit so I can speak the prophetic word. Instead, they reach out to receive, but are unwilling to give. They want what I give to them for free, but are unwilling to seek the Lord to supply my need. Isn't there something wrong with this picture?

Changing Our Perspective About Prophets and Prophecy

By and large, this describes how many in the church view prophetic ministry. They do not see it as an essential part of the church but as something that prophetic people do. In other words, what they say really doesn't matter. We don't need to hear from them; we can hear God for ourselves (Num. 12:2). This is the mindset in a large portion of the church today.

Recently some well-known leaders have spoken very harsh words about prophets, prophetic ministry, and prophetic people in general. They have shown their distaste for the ugly side of prophetic ministry, which I can understand. Yet at the same time, they have given the impression that they don't need prophetic ministry. In other words, they are saying they already have enough on their minds without having to deal with this prophecy thing.

This type of attitude is built upon the sinking sand of man's opinion rather than the solid rock of God's word (Mt. 7:24–27). It has done more damage to God's prophets through the centuries than anything else. Prophets have been stoned, beaten, bruised, and battered by those who have this philosophy. To them Jesus says, "…I will send them prophets and apostles, and some of them they shall slay and persecute: That the blood of all the prophets … may be required of this generation" (Lk. 11:49).

Would any of us want to stand before God with the blood of His holy prophets on our hands? Ouch! Yet when we despise prophetic ministry, abuse His prophetic servants, and slander their good names by our deceitfulness, we have opened the door to judgment in our own lives. God will not treat lightly those who treat His prophets poorly (Ps. 105:15). This is reality.

Living With an Eye on Eternity

We need a reality check here. We think God will do things our way and dance to our tune, but He does not. The Sovereign God will deal with us in His own way, and we better be ready to jump at His command. He may not speak to us a second time, and we may not get a second chance. Eternity may be only a heartbeat away. We could go before the judgment seat with the blood of the prophets on our hands.

I don't know about you, but as for me and my house, we will serve the Lord (Josh. 24:15). I am going to treat God's prophets well. Not that all of them have treated me well, but I choose to respect and believe in them rather than to mock or persecute them. I want to hear what God has to say through them, and to be open to whomever the Lord sends. I may not receive every prophetic word as from the Lord, but I will listen and test each one to determine if it is from Him (1 Thes. 5:21).

I will not casually throw away any prophetic word, even those I am unsure of. I may not see clearly at first what the real meaning is and how it applies to me. But I have come to the conclusion that prophecy speaks on a higher dimension than I can understand. Because of this, I like to meditate upon the prophetic words that I receive to see if they are from God and to determine exactly what He is saying to me. Only after I prove their accuracy will I act on these words.

Hearing What God is Really Saying

To act upon an unproven word is not wise, which is why I test those given to me. I like to see what they bring. First I like to test the fruit, which is how the word is working in my life (Mt. 7:16). If the fruit is good, then I know the word is good; otherwise, I take immediate steps to counteract any damage done by a false word. I commonly follow these procedures every time I receive a prophetic word from anyone, no matter how well known he or she is.

Learning how to deal with prophecy has not been as easy for me as it may sound. I have learned much of what I am writing here in the fires of experience. God has taught me what I know about prophecy by its work in my life. I have learned to tell the difference between a word from God, from the flesh, and from the devil. This has happened as I have struggled with learning to hear the voice of God.

Hearing God is not always as easy for prophets as one would imagine. Sometimes when I read the words of the prophets in the Bible, I wonder how God spoke to them. Was His voice audible, or did He silently speak to them in their hearts? Did they receive visions from God? If so, were the visions revealed openly or in their minds? We may never know the answers to these questions until we get to heaven. But the truth is that these holy men heard from God and they recorded what they heard for us (Heb. 1:1).

The Bible is a Prophetic Book

I like to think of the Bible as a heavenly tuning fork that enables us to be tuned in to God's voice. As we get closer to the voice of God, we harmonize with what God is speaking to us and what He has spoken to the prophets in the Bible. This is why the Word of

God is so important as a foundation for prophetic ministry. We all need to allow our ears to be tuned to the voice of God through His holy written word.

The work of prophecy begins in our own lives by hearing the word of God, for the testimony of Jesus is the Spirit of prophecy. This means that scripture itself is prophecy. As Paul said, "All scripture is given by inspiration of God" (2 Tim. 3:16). And Peter wrote, "For the prophecy [scriptures] came not in old time by the will of man: but holy men of God spake as they were moved by the Holy Ghost" (2 Pet. 2:21). The scriptures are prophetic in nature.

Therefore, the scriptures will do a prophetic work in our lives. When the word of God begins its work in us, it radically changes our lives. The scriptures describe this work of God as a circumcision of the heart, ears, and mouth (Is. 6:5, Jer. 6:10). This is what prepares us to be ready to do the work of the ministry in the arena of prophecy. God can use us because He can trust us to do what He has called us to do.

The Foundation for Ministry

This is the foundation for every ministry. Whether it is pastoral, evangelistic, or prophetic, we must be prepared through the scriptures for the work of service (2 Tim. 2:15). So we must allow the Holy Spirit to take us through periods of intense learning, both in the scriptures and through experience. As we learn and grow in our understanding of the calling of God upon our lives, then we are able to move into it. Once we move into the calling of God, we are ready to do the work of that calling.

The calling to speak prophetically is upon every believer, as God has given us the ability to speak on His behalf. Yet this does not make every believer a prophet for God. Nor does it mean that we have a gift of prophecy or that we have been assigned by the Holy Spirit to speak prophetically to the body. What it does mean is that all of us can prophesy the word of the Lord by the Holy Spirit to those around us because the church itself is prophetic.

Some Are Called to Prophesy

Within the church, however, God has set apart individuals to do the work of prophecy in the church. For some, this work may be in the local church; for others it may be outside of it. Some may be called to be prophets, and others to prophesy. Knowing the difference is not always as obvious as it might seem. Many prophets have not reached national acclaim, and others have. So I believe it is important for us to explore the types of prophecy in the body of Christ.

What are the different types of prophecy available to believers? You have probably heard of the prophet, which is actually an office within the church (Eph.

4:11). This is a governmental gift to the body of Christ. As Bill Hamon says, "The prophet is divinely endowed with the portion of Christ's gifting that made Him a prophet." This means that prophets obtain their gift from the person of Christ, and as such they have authority from Him to function in the church.

Many people have tried to argue against the office of prophet within the church. As such, I believe it is important to confront some of their inaccurate statements. I will deal with the fallacies about prophetic ministry that much of the church has come to accept as truth. Some of these are in the process of change, and some will be changed in the future as more revelation comes forth.

Questions and Answers About Prophets and Prophecy

First of all, are there prophets in the church? The answer is a hearty yes. Prophets have never been excluded from the model of ministry established by the early church fathers. Ignatius, one of the early church bishops, considered himself a prophet. He taught that the prophetic office was still in existence even though the apostles had been gone for almost 200 years. I am inclined to agree because he was a historical teacher of the church and because of the confirmation of the word.

Secondly, if prophets are in the church, should their words be considered equal with scripture? The obvious answer is no. No true prophet today would claim the authority to write scriptures. This is the only type of prophecy that is not available today to anyone under any circumstance. Anyone who claims otherwise is a false prophet. The scriptures are full and complete in their authority and integrity (Rev. 22:18,19).

Thirdly, if prophecy cannot be considered scripture, doesn't it mean that anyone who claims the title of prophet is false? No! The scriptures describe more then one type of prophecy. Many prophets are mentioned in scripture whose words were not recorded as such. Therefore, many prophetic words were spoken that were not considered scripture. The same is true today.

Fourthly, some have taught that prophets are still in the church, but have less authority than their Old Testament counterparts. In fact, prophets today have greater authority. Old Testament prophets were always separate from the leadership of Israel. New Testament prophets are considered part of the leadership of the church. For example, in Antioch, several New Testament prophets gathered to anoint Barnabas and Saul by the Holy Spirit as a new apostolic team (Acts 13:1).

Another false teaching today about prophets is that

they are to submit to pastoral authority. In fact, prophets and pastors are to be a team, anointed and appointed by Christ to govern the church. This problem has developed because the church has operated outside of Christ's authority for many years, being skewed toward a system not established by Him.

Another false teaching just beginning to arise is that prophets should be submitted to apostles. The problem with this teaching is that it contains a thread of truth: prophets should be submitted to apostles, but not in all cases (1 Cor. 12:28). To illustrate the fallacy behind this teaching, I will use an example. No one in his right mind would unilaterally or categorically tell pastors that they must submit to prophets, even though scripture declares that prophets have greater authority. Wouldn't that be foolish? Do you see what I am saying?

Relationship, not submission, is the standard for determining leadership boundaries. God sets those in authority as He wills, not as we will. God determines who is to submit to whom. First of all, He calls us to be submitted to Him (1 Pet. 5:5,6). This is how order is established in the church. Because of this, prophets *may* have greater authority than apostles, and pastors *may* have greater authority than prophets. Our man-made standards cannot be used to determine scriptural boundaries.

As Bill Hamon relates in his book, *Prophets and the*

Prophetic Movement, we cannot use different measures for different ministries. We cannot accuse prophets of doing what evangelists have been doing for years—ministering God's gifts of healing and salvation to the church and the world. Neither can we exclude prophets from their rightful place in the functioning church just because they are prophets. This would be the worst form of hypocrisy and heresy.

My purpose in writing about this is that we cannot single out the prophet to bring him into submission or under correction if we are not willing to play by the same rules. God condemns this. Speaking through the prophet Isaiah, He condemns this practice, telling Israel to repent for pointing their finger (Is. 58:9). I am doing the same here. If we are going to correct and discipline prophets, then we must be willing to allow God to correct and discipline all of us.

Why have I focused on the false teachings about prophets? Simply, these false teachings have done great damage to the prophet, prophetic ministry, and prophetic people. As a result, many who have been a blessing to the body of Christ have come under great bondage because we haven't been playing by our own rules. This may hurt, but it is time for someone to stand up and speak the truth, whether we like it or not.

Understanding the Gift of Prophecy

Along with the office of prophet, God has also provided the gift of prophecy to the church, which is from the Holy Spirit (1 Cor. 12:10). This means that the one speaking through the gift of prophecy reveals what the Holy Spirit desires for the church. The gift is usually used to edify, exhort, and comfort (1 Cor. 14:3). Unlike the prophet, the one with the gift of prophecy does not have the authority to establish church order or to give direction or guidance. They also do not speak governmentally or administratively.

The gift of prophecy can manifest itself in many forms, including dreams, visions, and revelations. The person with the gift of prophecy will be able to speak to many different groups of people. Yet their ministry is always one of revelation, not government. This is why they cannot be labeled as prophets.

Prophecy in the Church

The third type of prophecy in the church is what I call the body prophet (Rom. 12:6). This is a person assigned to minister in one particular church or denomination. He does not have governmental authority, nor does he have the ability to minister prophetically outside the body or denomination. As such, his sphere is limited to the place he has been called to by God—the local church or trans-local denomination.

The body prophet has been ordained by the Holy

Spirit to minister to the local church body to which he has been called. This will enable him to speak prophetically to people within the body for edification, exhortation, and comfort. In some cases, he will receive limited words about guidance and direction for the church or for people within the church. But the words he speaks will never be governmental in nature.

As you can see, God has given greatly diverse assignments to different members of His church for many reasons (1 Cor. 12:4–6). All are important and should be functioning in the church today. Every prophecy—whether through the prophetic office, the gift of prophecy, or body prophecy—is important for its own reasons and brings forth something beautiful in the eyes of God: a church under the influence of the spirit of prophecy. This is what we need in our day.

Giving and Receiving Prophecy With a Good Heart

We need prophecy that works. Not all of it does, often because the person giving or the one receiving doesn't do what is required to receive the anointing on the prophecy. We cannot prophesy without an anointing and then expect God's power to reside in our words (1 Cor. 12:3). We must seek the unction to serve in prophetic ministry if this is what we are called to do in Christ's body.

At the same time, people often come to receive prophetic ministry without preparing their hearts for the word to begin working in them (Mt. 13:23). They have preconceived notions of what God will or won't do. As such, they are not really willing to hear from God. They are not ready to hear prophecy that speaks of what they need in their lives but do not want. They come to prophets with idols in their hearts but have not been faithful with what they have been given (Ezek. 14:3).

Prophecy is not a toy; it works effectively on our behalf when used properly. Anyone who would throw out a prophecy because it doesn't fit within his frame of reference at the time is being very foolish. Also, prophets and prophetic people are foolish when they speak out of their own minds because they have not received God's anointing to function in power (Deut. 18:22). Just because we can flow in prophecy doesn't mean our prophecies are powerful.

More Love, More Power

Today's church needs powerful prophecy that works in us until the prophetic word is fulfilled. Samuel was one who was willing to pay the price to follow God. Because of this, he could hear the word of the Lord and see the release of God's work in his life. How many times has God's work suffered because a spoken prophecy had insufficient anointing? Or how many times has a prophecy been hindered from doing its work because our hearts were not right?

Prophecy must be understood as a tool in the hand of God for His work and will to be accomplished in us (John 6:63). Without it, certain things will not happen in our lives. It can release overnight what has been held back for years, or it can bring a vision of what God wants to do in the distant future (John 9:3,4).

A couple could be led into marriage through a clear word from the Lord. Prophecy may enable a childless couple to conceive. Many without prophecy will be bound by alcohol, drugs, sexual disorders, and the like. Prophecy accomplishes so many things on so many different levels that only prayer is comparable in its power. So prophecy and prayer must be of similar importance to believers.

Prophecy + Prayer = Power

I hope you hear what I am saying: in a very real sense, the value that we place on prayer should be the same as on prophecy. As prayer is vital to the Christian life, so too is prophecy. They both bring the hand of God into our lives, which we desperately need. As God's hand is extended to those who pray, so it is to those who receive prophecy. Those who receive and walk in the prophetic spirit will receive the benefit of that walk.

When we walk in the Spirit of prophecy and live in the realm of prayer, our spiritual lives shift into overdrive. Tasks that normally would take days, months, or years now take hours, days, or weeks. Think about it: one person operating in the Spirit can do more than hundreds or thousands of people operating in the flesh (Deut. 32:30). Prophecy has the power to energize, charge, and fill our spiritual batteries.

A Jewish Perspective of Prophecy

Many of the Jewish people understood the value of prophecy (Rom. 3:2). God used it to bring them into existence and to deliver them from bondage. He also used it to establish their worship, government, and laws. The Jewish people have spent thousands of years following prophecy, even though in many cases they have not understood or received it. So we need to understand prophecy from their perspective. When they spoke of prophecy, it was from their own cultural and theological background.

When the Jewish people spoke of prophecy, they used the word *dabar*, which describes what happens when a prophecy is given. When we see prophecy through the eyes of the Jewish people, their culture, language, and background, we more fully understand the power of prophecy. So understanding the meaning of the Hebrew word *dabar* is very important to receiving the work of prophecy.

Dabar—The Word of Prophecy

The word *dabar* means a word that sets something in motion or that is being driven to completion. It carries the notion that prophecy, when unhindered, is self-fulfilling. The prophetic word contains sufficient power to bring itself to completion. Nothing in the natural world, apart from our own actions, can stop prophecy from working in our lives.

Genuine prophecy from God subdues everything in our lives for the purpose of fulfilling the word. The prophetic word literally establishes and propels forward the kingdom of God in our lives. It establishes the dominion of God in the earth (Gen. 1:28).

Prophecy is a Weapon of War

The prophetic word is actually a declaration of war against the armies of darkness. When God speaks through prophetic people, the power structures of the enemy's kingdom can be disarmed and dismantled. This is why the devil hates prophecy so much—it destroys his kingdom while it builds the kingdom of God (Jer. 1:10). The prophetic word destroys everything that opposes it, and builds that which supports it.

When Jeremiah received his prophetic call from

God, he was told that his words would root out, pull down, destroy, throw down, build, and plant. God's plan for the prophetic word is for it to do a work. In fact, the reason God gives it to us is not just to give us information about who He is or what He will do, but also to assert His influence upon our lives to make sure it does happen. The prophetic word makes it easier for us to do God's will than not to do it.

Once we have this perspective of prophecy, it becomes meaningful when God speaks to us. Prophecy becomes more than just information or revelation—it becomes a power source for the anointing of God to flow into our lives so we can fulfill His will. Prophecy will work in, through, around and on us so we will become who God wants us to be. This is why all prophecy must be judged and understood correctly (1 Thes. 5:21).

Entering a Deeper Dimension in Prophecy

We need to know not only what the prophetic word says, but also what God sent it to do. This is where so many people fall short in the full release of the prophetic spirit. They assume that all prophecy is the same, when in reality it isn't. The prophetic word can do many different things in our lives. As such, we need to know what the word of prophecy was sent to do before we can fully enter into it.

Chapter Three

The Word of Prophecy

"Hold fast the form of sound words, which thou has heard of me, in faith and love which is in Christ Jesus. That good thing which was committed unto thee keep by the Holy Ghost which dwelleth in us."
2 Tim. 1:13,14

The prophetic word is powerful—it can do a great work, as we saw in the last chapter. It has the ability to breathe life into us (Gen. 2:7). We are touched and renewed by the Holy Spirit through the prophetic word as it enables us to serve Christ with all our hearts. As such, the word of prophecy is designed to release a greater commitment to the purposes of Christ in and through our lives.

I love the prophetic word. I have been greatly ministered to by personal prophecy. When God has spoken to me prophetically, huge doors of opportunity have often been opened. I am grateful for the faithful men and women who have ministered to me prophetically. To them I want to say "thank you." You have played a great part in the work that God has called me to do. Through you I have been healed, blessed, built up, held up, and comforted. You have corrected and directed me into God's plan for my life.

The prophetic word should build us up and bless us. It should give us a sense of being touched by God's hand (Ezek. 3:14). God has the ability to do more through one word than we could accomplish in a lifetime of activity. This is the power behind the prophetic word, and this is why we so desperately need it in our day. We need to be touched by the hand of our Savior, Jesus Christ.

Prophecy Can Restore Us

With all that is happening in the world, we need a clear word from heaven. The enemy is seeking to overwhelm the church with his filth (Rev. 12:15). Crime is running rampant, humanity has lost its sanity, our souls have been scarred, and our consciences seared. We can no longer determine what is right or wrong, good or evil, just or unjust. This is not only scary—it shows the level of depravity that humanity has suffered through our fallen condition (Rom. 1:20–32). We have fallen from grace, and His creation has been corrupted by our fall.

The prophetic word is one of the main tools that God uses to restore our lost grace and dignity. Through the word of prophecy, He imparts grace to us by which we can live for Him in this chaos of corruption. His grace is sufficient for us once we receive it (2 Cor. 12:9). But in truth, many of us have not known how to receive the grace necessary to live for Him.

The word of prophecy is a conduit of grace and mercy (1 Pet. 1:10). God uses it to impart His nature, character, plan, purpose, and design for our lives. We receive a word that imparts to us something that we did not have and could not receive on our own. Prophecy is important to the church—it saves us from ourselves and from the lost condition of those around us. Praise God for the prophetic word!

Prophecy: The Divine Catalyst

The word of prophecy is quickening and life-giving; it flows through the Holy Spirit into our hearts and releases great blessing and joy (Lk. 1:46,47). It releases the flow of grace from the Holy Spirit that we so desperately need to live in this world. All of us need this, from the newest believer to the oldest saint. We need to be touched personally by the hand of God through the vehicle of prophecy.

When this happens, many gifts are released into our lives that would otherwise be lacking (Gen. 1:3). Prophecy will bring faith, hope, and love where none exists. It will bring grace, mercy, and peace where more is needed. The prophetic word will bring finances, healing, and deliverance where our need is greatest. It will bring all of these gifts and more into our lives.

Prophecy equips, empowers, and enables us to fulfill the will of God. It is a divine spark and activator for what He desires to do in our lives. When we receive prophecy, a world of possibility is opened up to us that will help us overcome confusion and doubt (Dan. 5:16). We will have confidence in our ability to do what God is speaking to our hearts because we know God is standing behind us. Prophecy confirms to our hearts who the Father is in our lives.

Knowing the Father

The word of prophecy reveals the nature of God to our hearts. We see the Father as He is, not as who we think Him to be. He opens our eyes to see the love that He has for us, and how intimately He knows us.

God is watching us as we live our lives for Him, and is protecting us from the evil one (Ps. 34:7). He is speaking to His angels about what His sons and daughters are doing on planet earth. The Father is rejoicing over us with great joy.

This is why the Bible declares to us that God is singing and dancing over us (Zeph. 3:17). He delights in who He made us to be. To us the Father says, "I know the thoughts that I think toward you, thoughts of peace, and not of evil, to give you an expected end" (Jer. 29:11). He also says, "You are fearfully and wonderfully made" (Ps. 139:14). Is this how you see yourself and those around you? This is who we are and what we are called to be. And the word of prophecy enables us to become all this and more.

The prophetic word is a source of many great things. Therefore, let us delve into the scriptures to see what they are about and what the prophetic word will do in our lives (2 Tim. 2:15). As we look into what the Bible says about prophecy, I think you will be surprised at how much the word of prophecy can do in our lives.

The Ultimate Prophecy

All scripture can rightly be called prophecy, but not all prophecy can be called scripture (2 Tim. 3:16, 2 Pet. 1:19–21). This one simple truth can save us a lot of heartache as we deal with the prophetic word in our lives. We should never treat any prophecy we receive today with the same authority that we give to the Bible. The holy scriptures are a type of prophecy that is no longer being given today. It is what the Bible calls the prophecy of scripture.

The canon of scripture is complete in every way; it is the full revelation of God to humanity. Its pages contain the blueprint of God's master plan for all of humanity and the nations of the world. It includes the key to salvation and the way to heaven. It is the roadmap to the fullness of God's plan for everyone. This is why we need to read, study, and apply the scriptures to our lives.

The word of prophecy is never to be held in the same authority as that of scripture. So if any prophecy contradicts what is written or claims to be an addition to scripture, it should not be received but disregarded. Many of the cults today—such as the Mormons, Freemasons, Jehovah's Witnesses, and Christian Scientists—have taken, twisted, or added to the body of the scriptures. They have done this to their own destruction (2 Pet. 3:16).

Avoiding Heresy

Whenever we add to or take away from the scriptures, we are on thin ice with God. This is why so much of the church is in trouble today—we have cherry-picked the word of God. We thought we could obtain God's promises without walking in God's standards. This lie is from the pit of hell and has caused the church to depart from the truths of the faith (Jude 1:3). We have come to accept things that are not only blatantly unscriptural, but things that are evil at their core.

The church that turns away from the prophecy of scripture is walking the highway to hell. Many have fallen into this trap of the devil, including great men and women of God. The road to heaven is lined with stories of those who have become shipwrecked in their faith (1 Tim. 1:19,20). Their great gifts could not sustain them and bring them into the fullness of what Jesus desired to do in their lives. They lost their foundation of the holy scripture and began to build upon a foundation of sinking sand.

The Bible says, "Now all these things happened unto them for examples: and they are written for our admonition, upon whom the ends of the world are come. Wherefore let him that thinketh he standeth take heed lest he fall" (1 Cor. 10:11,12). This is a sober warning of the consequences of selling out to the lies of the devil. We need the scriptures so that we can set our hearts aright with God and be steadfast in our spirits with Him.

What Prophecy Can Do for You

Prophecy can never be a substitute for the scriptures in our lives. We need to desire the sincere milk of the word of God so that we do not become spoiled through the prophecies that we receive (1 Pet. 2:2). The prophetic word, if not balanced in our lives by the scriptures, has the ability to puff us up into arrogant, prideful people instead of humble, submitted servants to Christ. The only way to avoid this is by allowing God to lay a solid foundation of His word in our lives.

As such, I want to discuss the foundation that God is seeking to lay in our lives, both through the written word of God and through the word of prophecy. The scriptures declare to us what attributes God's word can release into our lives. These attributes are the same as those released through the prophetic word. The importance of prophecy is that it releases something to us that we have not had prior to the time we received it.

What does prophecy release to us? According to the scriptures, both the written word and the word of prophecy release exhortation, salvation, grace, promise, wisdom, knowledge, reconciliation, truth, life, power, righteousness, the oath (covenant), prophecy, and patience. I will now talk about each of these things specifically.

Exhortation, Salvation and Grace

The word of prophecy will release into our lives a sense of exhortation (Acts 13:15, Heb. 13:22). We will have an urgency in our hearts upon receiving prophetic ministry. We will know that God is calling us to change certain areas of our lives. He will warn us about things that are coming and help us stay on track. We will know that God has given us His advice about situations we are facing. This will release to us God's wisdom and deliverance into our lives.

The word of prophecy will release salvation into our lives (1 Pet. 1:10). It will save, heal, and deliver us as well as our families. Prophecy can bring us into a realm of salvation like nothing else can. It can touch us and our families, jobs, marriages, ministries, and more.

The word of prophecy has the ability to release God's grace into our lives (Acts 20:32). After receiving prophecy, we will be charged by the power of God. His ability will be released to us so that we can become what the prophetic word says we will be. The door will be opened so we may enter into God's will for our lives, and we will have the grace necessary to walk through it.

Promise, Wisdom and Knowledge

The word of prophecy will release a sense of promise (Rom. 9:9). We will know that God has given us His word concerning areas in our lives that are important to us. This understanding releases faith and grace to live for Him in this present world. We will have hope and understanding of what God is doing based upon covenant—the foundation for real faith. It is this foundation that will release God's blessing and provision to us.

The word of prophecy has the potential to release the wisdom of God into our lives (1 Cor. 12:8). The wisdom that we lack will be supplied through the prophetic word. When this happens, we will be able to live our lives circumspectly. Our time will be well managed and will be focused on the objective that God has given to us. We will not waste our time on unfruitful endeavors, but will be able to bear much fruit to the glory, honor, and praise of His name.

The word of prophecy can release supernatural knowledge into our lives (1 Cor. 12:8). Things we are not aware of at the time we receive a prophecy will come to light. Answers to questions about calling, destiny, purpose, and provision will be met. God will give us specific knowledge of the fact that He is watching over us. This may even include specific information about our lives—where we live, who we know, what we do, or what will happen in the future. All these things and more can happen in prophecy.

Reconciliation, Truth, and Life

The word of prophecy is one way that God can release reconciliation into the hearts of His people (2 Cor. 5:19). Often God will call us to be reconciled to

Him and to one another through the vehicle of prophecy. It is powerful and can release us from the chains of bondage that have held us captive to hatred, bitterness, envy, strife, debate, and deceit. These chains are dissolved in the light of God's prophetic word, and forgiveness is freely released to flow through our hearts.

The word of prophecy is a powerful avenue for God to release truth to us (Col. 1:5). Often our eyes are closed to the obvious, and the only way God can break through is by the vehicle of prophecy. When this happens, the prophetic word releases us from the deception of the enemy. This can happen to one individual or to an entire nation, depending upon the anointing of the prophetic word and its messenger. Martin Luther King is a tremendous example of this kind of release of prophetic truth.

The word of prophecy can release the life of God to us (1 John 1:1). A major quality of prophecy is that it should have life. The abundant life of God flows through prophecy. It brings us into a new dimension. New doors open, new relationships start, and new gifts are released. It makes us feel alive, and the death in us is swallowed up by the life in the prophetic word.

Miracles, Righteousness and Covenant

The word of prophecy often releases the miracle-working power of God (Heb. 1:3). Suffering, sickness, and sin cannot stand against the prophetic word. Many people who have suffered for years will be healed or delivered instantaneously. The prophetic word releases God's power. Financial miracles will take place. The heavens will be opened, and the blessing of God will pour out upon us. Things that would have taken years will happen in a matter of moments. This is the wonderful power of prophecy.

The word of prophecy will enable us to walk in the way of righteousness (Heb. 5:13). We will know how to walk before God and will hunger for His ways. Our lives will be radically aligned with His purposes for us. We will know what to do and how to do it. Hindrances and barriers that have kept us from fully following God will fall as righteousness is released through the prophetic word.

The word of prophecy should release to us an understanding of the covenant (Heb. 7:28). We should know God who made the covenant with us, and understand the covenant the Father made with the Son. When this happens, we will see the redemptive work of prophecy released into and through our lives. Prophecy will open to us the power resident in the redemptive work of Christ at the cross.

Prophecy and Patience

The word of prophecy will often release the spirit of prophecy upon our lives (2 Pet. 2:19). We will have the ability to prophesy where we didn't before. The prophecies we receive will make way for the prophetic word to be given through us. God will pour out the grace to prophesy upon our lives. His spirit will enter into the midst of a congregation to such a degree that everyone present will be able to prophesy.

The word of prophecy should give us the grace necessary to be patient (Rev. 3:10). I know that doesn't sound like fun, but it is essential for the fulfillment of the prophecies we receive. Prophecy requires patience, so God will release the grace necessary to walk in the fruit of patience. When this happens, it releases us from the pressure of busyness within the world system. We are able to cast all our cares upon the Lord, and as a result are freed fully into His will.

These are things that prophecy can and should release into our lives. Power is resident in the word of prophecy that we as believers are called to tap into, especially those prophesying. Not every prophecy will contain all the things I have mentioned, but every prophecy will contain some of these things if they are from the Lord. So we need to study the prophecies that we receive to clearly determine what the Lord is saying to us. This will open us up to what God wants to impart into our lives.

The Unfolding Drama of Prophecy

Prophecy is more than just a word from God—it is

an impartation of His divine nature and character into our lives (2 Pet. 1:3,4). Prophecy can transform us from what we are into what God wants us to be. When this happens, this transformation can be as dramatic as that of a caterpillar turning into a butterfly. We need this type of unfolding drama in the church. We are to be a church that is constantly changing into the image of Jesus. And how awesome this truly can be!

This is why the Bible encourages us to be ready to give and receive the word and spirit of prophecy in our lives. God has designed us to go from glory to glory, faith to faith, grace to grace, and strength to strength. Prophecy can and does help us do this, which is why we need it in the church. We cannot be what God has called us to be without prophecy. Prophecy is essential to the health and life of the normal church—we desperately need this precious gift in our churches today.

Because of this, I want to charge you by God's anointed word: "Receive the Holy Spirit of prophecy."

Chapter Four

The Hearing Ear and Seeing Eye

"The hearing ear, and the seeing eye, the Lord hath made even both of them."
Prov. 20:12

God is the author and finisher of our faith. He enables us to connect with Him on His level. We need God's help to be able to hear or see what He is doing. Often we miss His deeds because we do not seek Him. So we must learn how to seek God for a hearing ear and a seeing eye, for He is the one who provides them.

I believe it is the desire of God's heart to communicate with us, but not just at our level, which He is often forced to do because of our hardness of heart. Our Father in heaven wants to communicate with us at His level. He wants to raise us to a new place in our ability to communicate. For this to happen, we must be willing to receive the language in which He wants to communicate with us.

The language of God is not the same as that of man (Is. 55:8,9). God speaks at a profoundly deeper level than we can ever understand, using a totally different language from our own. No wonder we have such a difficult time understanding God—we must learn His language. This is the crux of this chapter.

Learning How God Speaks

The language of God comes through many vehicles, including prophecy. He has chosen to speak to man through this channel. This means that when God does speak to us through the prophecy, we must listen carefully to what He is saying because it may not always be clear. This is where our patience comes in—we must be willing to learn the language of God (Heb. 10:36).

Learning the language of God doesn't happen overnight, and most of us aren't born with the gift of interpreting it. We must learn His language before we can clearly understand Him. This may take some time. If we were to learn a human language, it could take months or years, depending on the time and effort we put into it. The same is true as we seek to learn God's language.

Why should we want to learn the language of God? Because what God is saying is infinitely more valuable than what anyone else could possibly say. Everything He communicates to us via His Spirit is worth more than gold, silver, rubies, or any other precious metal or stone (Prov. 3:15). Hearing from God is as vital to our spiritual survival as bread, water, and air are for our physical survival.

Prophets are valuable to the church because they hear what God is saying. It is this ability to hear God that makes them special in His eyes. God treasures His prophets because they are the channels through which He is able to speak to His people. This is why we need them. They are the eyes and ears of the body of Christ on earth, so they are able to see and hear what God is saying to us in His language.

Why We Need Prophets and Prophecy

We need prophets and prophetic people. A church without them is deaf, dumb, and blind, making it difficult to communicate with God. Not that we don't want to talk with or hear from Him—of course we do. The problem is that we are prevented from hearing God as clearly as we should. Prophets bring the healing balm of God to pour upon our eyes, ears, and mouths so we can hear and talk with God (Jer. 8:22).

Prayer becomes much richer with a prophetic element in it. Most of the time, our prayer lives become dull because we are dull of hearing, and we don't seek out prophets who can help us hear from God. We need to surround ourselves with those who do hear from Him. They can become a tremendous asset to our walk with God and our spiritual survival as saints.

I wonder how many believers have failed in their spiritual lives because they didn't surround themselves with men and women who could hear from God. They were golden prospects for the kingdom of God, but they traded in their glittering crowns of Christ's matchless wealth for the fool's gold of man's opinion. What a way to end one's spiritual race—blind, bankrupt, and broken. Yet this is how too many of God's people end it. They become shipwrecked on the sinking sand of man's opinion (Mt. 7:24–27).

This is why we need to learn how to hear what God is saying. We must lay aside the natural things and pick up the eternal things of the Spirit (1 Cor. 2:14). We will still live in the natural, but our focus will be on the spiritual. It is as we do this that our spiritual lives will have new meaning. The voice of God will become clear, and we will hear what He is saying to us for such a time as this.

Becoming Dependent on God

This should be the attitude of the church, yet in most cases it isn't. We have gone far too long without the help of God. Somehow we think that we can do what we should without Him. This is especially true in the area of prayer. We don't recognize our utter dependence upon Him. We are so full of ourselves that we are prevented from seeing that we don't know how to pray to receive results. Yet answered prayer is the culmination of a heart yielded to the Father (1 John 5:14,15).

This is why it is important for us to hear that we don't know how we should pray (Rom. 8:26). Our language cannot even come close to touching the Father's heart without the Holy Spirit's help. Even our best attempts at prayer fall short. So we are utterly dependent upon God when we pray.

The scriptures are certainly true in saying that when we are weak, we are truly strong through His sufficient grace. This is the blessing of being a believer in Jesus Christ. We are on the cutting edge of those who are seeking to know Him. It is in knowing Him that we are changed into His image (1 John 3:2). Our words become His words, and our thoughts His thoughts. We are changed from what we once were into what God wants us to become.

This is the power of language. Few things can wield power like words can. The old saying goes, "the pen is mightier than the sword," and yet in the realm of history, the pen has often become a sword. According to James, "the tongue is a fire, a world of iniquity ... that setteth on fire the course of nature; and it is set on fire of hell" (James 3:6) Sin defiles the tongue and makes it unclean.

When Isaiah saw God, he said, "Woe is me! for I am undone; because I am a man of unclean lips, and I dwell in the midst of a people of unclean lips: for mine eyes have seen the King, the Lord of hosts" (Is. 6:5). Oh, for a vision like Isaiah's that would root out the slander, accusation, gossip, and fault finding in the body of Christ. We need a hot coal from the altar of God to cleanse our tongues; only then we will have eyes to see and ears to hear.

Being in Covenant With God

Having hearing ears and seeing eyes is directly related to our tongues being cleansed in the sight of God. No wonder the scriptures plead with us to allow Him to cleanse our tongues (Is. 1:16). And yet they call us to an even higher degree of communication—they call for our tongues to be circumcised. Talk about pain! And yet we must do this if we are to see into the realm of the Spirit and learn to communicate with God in His language.

Circumcision is always a sign of covenant. Our covenant with God is only as strong as our willingness to be set apart for Him through the process of circumcision. This is not the circumcision of the Old Testament, which was a symbol of the cleansing of man's seed, but the circumcision of the heart, eyes, ears, and mouth. We need to allow God to cleanse us in these areas, for they destroy our covenant with God and others. We can only live in covenant to the degree that we use our words as agents of blessing.

I have met many people who claimed they were in covenant with God or others, but their mouths betrayed them. They belittled their spouses, churches, friends, parents, and leaders. They broke their covenant because they could not keep themselves in the place of circumcision. Their eyes wandered, they listened to things that they shouldn't, and they said things that were unclean. They became adulterers and adulteresses, friends of the world, and enemies of God (James 4:4). What an awful way to live as a believer.

Heaven is Listening

Our words really do count. Sticks and stones may break our bones, but our words will live with us eternally. We will be judged according to what we say and how we say it. God will hold us accountable for every idle word that we utter (Mt. 12:36). This means that when Judgment Day rolls around—and by the way, it's just around the corner—we will be judged accordingly. For some of us, this could spell disaster or worse.

What you say is a reflection of who you are. Who you are is influenced by what you see and hear. Do you pay enough attention to what you see and hear? I know I don't. I am guilty, just like you, of watching and listening to things I shouldn't. For example, many times I know I should turn off the TV, but I don't. These worldly influences affect us whether we realize it or not. The results may not be immediate, but they are eternal. Eventually they will come out of our mouths if we allow enough negative input through our eyes and ears.

Hearing from God requires us to cleanse our tongues as well as our eyes and ears. The Father really does watch what we do (Prov. 5:21). This can be both frightening and comforting. He knows everything we do, whether for good or evil. He knows what is on our minds and what we will say next. God knows everything we do from the moment we rise in the morning until we close our eyes at night.

We certainly would change our tune if we knew that God was listening. Our tongues wouldn't wag against others as often as they do. We would use our words sparingly, knowing our Master in heaven listens to every jot and tittle. Just think about how every word is being recorded. Imagine the overwhelming accounting job the angels must have in writing down everything we say. One day those books will be opened (Rev. 20:12).

No wonder Isaiah said, "Woe is me; I am a man of unclean lips." Even as a prophet, Isaiah allowed sin to slip into His tongue. The prophet's tongue was to be a picture of purity, completely cleansed from guile, deceit, envy, bitterness, and strife—but it wasn't. Isaiah was a sinner just like the people around him. His tongue kept him from living a holy life, but he didn't even know it. It took a divine revelation through a visitation for him to discover it.

Purity is Important in Prophecy

Holiness doesn't automatically come with being a prophet. Having the ability to call strangers by name doesn't necessarily mean that one's tongue has been cleansed from sin. And the sins of the tongue are the most devastating; they grip all of mankind, including the church. So our tongues must be circumcised, especially those of God's prophets. We must allow God to do a work in our tongue so that He can do a work in our lives.

This is the call upon the church: a progressive work of circumcision, first of the heart, then the tongue, then the ears, and finally the eyes. It is purity in all that we hear, say, and do that makes us fit for service to the king (2 Tim. 2:20). We are ready to speak His word because we have come into the place of holiness in Him. His word of circumcision in us causes us to become connected through covenant.

This is what the body of Christ is all about. We are called to be a body of believers who love God and one another in word, thought, and deed. Yet for this to happen, we must come to a place of brokenness in Him. We must allow God to do a work in us. Our words and lives must be replaced by His. He must increase, but we must decrease. Our death prepares the way for His life (2 Cor. 1:9). The cross of Christ is applied in our lives through the circumcision of our hearts, mouths, ears, and eyes.

This is the foundation for living the Christian life. I am sharing with you the rudimentary principles of discipleship as revealed in scripture (Heb. 5:12). To the degree these principles are not being taught in the church or implemented in our lives, we have strayed from the truth as it is found in Jesus. Seeing and hearing what God is saying doesn't come cheaply. No! There is a price to pay to see and hear what God is saying, and this price is our willingness to lay down our lives in simple obedience to the principles of Christ.

Samuel: A Godly Example to Follow

Are you ready? Are you willing to lay down your life to pick up Christ's? Do you want to see and hear what God is saying? If so, you have just started the most important journey in this life. You have decided to enter into the realm of prophecy. You are seeking to communicate with God on His terms and in His language. What an awesome adventure and dangerous journey this can be. Many trials, troubles, and tribulations will try to prevent you from entering into this place of prophecy. Yet I want to encourage you—don't let them keep you out. You can enter into all that God has for you.

This is what Samuel did during the days of Eli the priest. Eli's family had corrupted the priesthood in Israel. The scripture says that no open vision existed in those days (1 Sam. 3:1). A famine of hearing and seeing the word of the Lord was in the land (Amos 8:11). And yet Samuel, because he walked circumspectly before the Lord, heard and saw what God was saying to such a degree that none of his words fell to the ground (1 Sam. 3:19). What a testimony for a prophet—total victory in every area of life.

Samuel brought in the prophetic priesthood that could hear and see what God was saying. This is what God is doing in our day. For too long we have been blind and deaf; the time has come for the church to see and hear. You are a part of the mighty army of prophetic priests who can hear and see what God is saying (1 Pet. 2:9). The time has come for this army to be released on an unsuspecting world. It's our turn now!

Lift Your Voice Like a Trumpet

Talk about conflict—we haven't seen anything yet.

God's army of prophetic priests is going to take hold of this world and turn it back toward a holy God. He will be seen in His holiness. The church will be seen in her righteousness. And this army will be seen in its fullness, carrying forth the word of the Lord. How awesome is the army that carries forth the banner of Christ's victory (Song 6:4). They will rush on the city and run on the walls as they carry forth His word.

We live in an awesome day of God's power. He will judge and make war against the nations of the earth (Rev. 19:11). We are a part of His awesome army waging this warfare. And we will not rest until we have victory. Yet we can be assured of this, for we know we are on the Lord's side (Josh. 5:13–15).

Lift up your voice like a trumpet and call for all to come to the table of the Lord and partake of that which money cannot buy. Those in the world would give everything they own to have what we have—the pearl of great price, the Son of God, our Lord Jesus Christ. We are emissaries of His presence and ambassadors of His love. Our eyes and ears are opened to the sound of heaven above.

Hear the joyful sound as Christ's voice fills the earth. As the scriptures say, "the earth shall be filled with the knowledge of the glory of the Lord as the waters cover the sea" (Is. 11:9). We will be the ones in our generation who have our eyes and ears opened. Our tongues will be cleansed to speak and our minds will be renewed to think thoughts from above. We will learn the language of God through prophecy and enter the realm of covenant through circumcision of the heart, tongue, ears, and eyes.

We have arrived to the kingdom just in time for such a time as this—get ready and go for it!

Chapter Five

As Dew in the Morning

"Therefore God give thee of the dew of heaven, and the fatness of the earth, and plenty of corn and wine: Let people serve thee, and the nations bow down to thee: be lord over thy brethren, and let thy mother's sons bow down to thee: cursed be everyone that curseth thee, and blessed be he that blesseth thee."

Gen. 27:28

In 1987, God called me into the prophetic ministry. At that time I had almost no understanding of how to hear His voice. Christianity was new to me. I didn't grow up in the church and had never really attended one. The church itself was a mystery to me. Sometimes I liked it, and sometimes I didn't. I had met some really weird people there. Many of them lived respectable lives except when they came to church, where they did some really dumb things.

This was my introduction into the world of prophecy. I thought goosebumps on my arms were good and hair standing on the back of my head was bad. Shaking was a sure sign to me that God was present. I didn't have a clue as to how to hear from God or to know if He was speaking to me. Even today, after ministering prophetically to thousands of individuals, I still sometimes have the question: Was that really God?

Leaving the Twilight Zone

Has this ever happened to you? If so, you have been in the twilight zone of prophetic ministry, where not everything is as it seems. I have seen some of the sanest people do some of the most insane things in the name of prophetic ministry. Sometimes you wonder if their minds have gone blank. Some claim that they are hearing God when in reality they are hearing their own sinful imaginations, or even worse, the devil.

The prophetic ministry has a dark side, and few are willing to talk about it. Rather, many are quick to condemn it while they overlook the failures in the church today among her leaders (Acts 3:19). The truth is that we have failed miserably at doing what the Bible says we are called to do, which is to live by every word that proceeds from the mouth of God (Mt. 4:4).

The calling upon the life of every Christian is to live by what God says to us individually and corporately. So why have we failed so miserably? Where is the sure word of prophecy in our midst (2 Pet. 1:19)? Where is the clarion call that can help us discern the heavenly sound of God's voice on the earth? Why have we settled for something far less than this, and trained people to do the same? Maybe it's time that we account for what we have and haven't done.

Shattering Our Illusions

Reflection can be a good thing, as long as it leads us to repentance—a place so few of us are really willing to enter. This means death to the "my way or the highway" mentality permeating the church today. No wonder people are leaving church in droves—we have driven them away with our superficial, carnal gospel. We have misled people into believing things that aren't true in the name of greed and false glory. It's time that we look in the mirror to see where we are with God (James 1:24,25).

The mirror of God can be a healing place if we

allow it to become so. It can remove our false impressions about who we are and shatter the illusions we have of one another. Mirages fade in the mirror of God. We start to see clearly and perceive God's reality. His mirror breaks the power and influence of idols that hold us in bondage to the world's ways (1 John 5:21).

Removing Idols from the Church

I believe that one of the greatest sins in the church today is idolatry. We have marketed artificial images of men and women of God. We have presented false notions about who we are in the hope of selling ourselves to the body of Christ. Men have been exalted at the expense of Christ. The biggest problem is that we think it is acceptable to be this way. We don't even realize that God's glory has departed from our lives (1 Sam. 4:21). Like Samson, the Spirit has left us and we are unaware of it.

How sad it is that someone could be born of the Spirit, and yet fade away into a place of fleshly indulgence and greed (Gal. 3:3). And yet this is what many are doing today in the name of God. Few are willing to stand up and speak about what is going on in the church today. The fear of man has held the church in bondage to idols of men. It's no wonder that so many have wandered out of the way. We have been following dumb idols and not Christ.

It is time to break the silence. The voice of God must be heard. A generation is longing for God to speak in truth and deed. They will not be denied. We must prepare the way for them to hear what God is really saying. To do this, we must cast down the idols of men in the house of God. The time has come for judgment to begin, and this is where it will begin (1 Pet. 4:17). God is about to clean His house of the idols that we have built up in His name.

Fear God, Live Wisely, Listen Carefully

Get ready! God is about to visit His house (Amos 4:12). The time of our visitation is at hand. God will pass through our midst (Amos 5:17). There will be weeping, wailing, and howling. The church will know that God is in heaven, ruling in the affairs of men (Dan. 4:32). We will see who He really is, and we will realize the fear of the Lord in our hearts (Prov. 9:10). This will enable us to hear the voice of wisdom in the coming days.

We need wisdom in this hour (Prov. 4:7). We need to learn how to hear from God and to apply what we hear. We need to know what God is saying and how to walk in it with wisdom. Because of this, we must know God's ways (Ps. 103:7). Understanding His ways enables us to walk with wisdom in His word. Without this balanced approach to living in God's kingdom, we could get sidetracked or even sidelined in the coming days.

As we approach the end of the world, it will become increasingly important to hear the voice of God. How can we learn to hear God's voice? By allowing what He has said to build a solid foundation for our understanding of the voice of God. What God is saying now will always be consistent with what He has said in the past. His words are the building blocks upon which are formed the ABC's of the language of God.

The ABC's of God's Language

The Bible says, "God ... hath in these last days spoken to us by His Son" (Heb. 1:1,2). Jesus is the fullest expression of the voice of God ever revealed on earth (John 1:14). Because of this, I believe the gospels are foundational in their importance. Through them we can accurately hear the voice of God, for they reveal the person of Christ to us. The life of Jesus is expressed fully in the gospels. We see who Jesus was and who He is today. We see what Jesus did and what He will do today. We hear what Jesus said and what He will say today. The gospels are foundational, but they are not the complete foundation.

The Bible itself is the single greatest literary work ever created. God Himself is its author. As we read it, our minds are changed and we catch a glimpse into things that are unseen. We see the mysteries of God that have been hidden since the fall of mankind. Through its pages, we read of His unspeakable glory. Things unexplainable are explained. We catch a glimpse of the hidden realm of the heart whereby we see the love God has for us (John 3:16). What love!

Paul said, "All scripture is given by inspiration of God, and is profitable for doctrine, for reproof, for correction, for instruction in righteousness: That the man of God may be perfect, thoroughly furnished unto all good works" (2 Tim. 3:16,17). The Bible is the map we can follow to find the will of God for our lives, and it is within our reach every day. We just have to pick it up and read it. No wonder the enemy fights so hard against it. It is the complete, inerrant, inspired, and holy Word of God.

Not only has God spoken to us through His Son and His Word, but He has also chosen to speak to us through creation. Listen to what the Bible says about the creation: "The heavens declare the glory of God; and the firmament sheweth His handywork. Day unto day uttereth speech, and night unto night sheweth knowledge. There is no speech or language where there voice is not heard. Their line is gone out through all the earth, and their words to the ends of the world" (Ps. 19:1–4).

God has chosen to communicate with all of mankind throughout the ages by creation. Creation sings the songs of God and reveals the mysteries of who He is. We see God's character through nature. Even in its fallen state, the world today is a constant reminder of God. As Paul said, "The invisible things of Him are clearly seen, being understood by the things that are made, even His eternal power and Godhead; so that they are without excuse" (Rom. 1:20).

God's voice can be heard today through what He has already said through His Son, His Word, and creation. These are just some of the foundational ways that God has spoken to us. When we hear from God through them, we are hearing what God has said already. This lays a solid foundation for us to hear what God is saying today. It is critical that we understand what God has said through these various means so that we can hear what He is saying now.

Prophets Can Help Us Hear God

The reason for saying all of this is to lay a foundation for what I will say from this point forward. I want to help you understand when and how God speaks today. We have already seen that God wants us to see and hear, and that certain individuals in the body of Christ have been given the ability to help us do this. They are the eyes and ears of the body of Christ. The prophetic ministry is all about helping us hear and see what God is saying.

God desires to speak to us. He has proven this by

already doing so in many different ways. Not only this, but He desires for us to hear Him. We were all made to hear His voice. Every single person in the world has this ability. No one has been left out because of race, creed, or color. Everyone is included, and everyone is invited to hear from the God, the Sovereign King of the universe.

Just think about that for a moment. We were all made to hear from God. He wants to speak to us, and He knows our language. He made the way for us to hear from Him (Heb. 6:19,20). The problem is that few of us know how. We don't recognize Him when He speaks because we are not used to His voice. So when He does speak, we often tune Him out.

The prophetic voice is important to the church because it helps us tune in to what God is saying. Prophets by nature have an uncanny ability to tune in to the voice of God, regardless of what may be happening around them. Their words resonate with the voice of God. Their thoughts accentuate and give expression to the thoughts of God.

The voice of God is released through prophets in several different ways. For some it may be through visions. For others, it may be through their voices, or through inward thought patterns or processes. These are all part of the prophetic voice and gifting that God gives. Yet I believe one in particular has been overlooked by the majority of the prophetic community. This prophecy comes as the rain, and I believe is representative of the spirit of prophecy.

Releasing the Spirit of Prophecy

The Hebrew word for this type of prophecy is *Nataf*, which literally means to fall like rain from heaven. It is found 21 times in the Old Testament. The word describes the prophetic voice coming as the rain, bringing a fresh scent of the voice of heaven. This type of prophecy is so powerful because it is not localized as the other prophetic revelations are, nor is it dependent upon the prophet Himself. It speaks to a wider group of people, bringing greater revelation, through the prophetic flow.

Moses was speaking of this type of prophecy when he said, "Give ear, O ye heavens, and I will speak; and hear, O earth, the words of my mouth. My doctrine shall drop as the rain, my speech shall distill as the dew, as the small rain upon the tender herb, and as the showers upon the grass…" (Deut. 32:1,2). God is not speaking through one individual to many, but to many individuals by one Spirit. This is the Spirit of prophecy in operation on earth.

Amos, speaking of the same type of Spirit of prophecy, wrote, "The Lord God hath spoken, who can but prophesy?" (Amos 3:8). This means that when the Spirit of prophecy falls upon a particular location, everyone present will come under its influence. An example of this would be when Saul sent his men to Samuel's school of prophets. They all came under the influence of the spirit of prophecy to such a degree that they prophesied (1 Sam. 19:20–24).

The Spirit of prophecy can be an irresistible force for the expansion of God's kingdom. When the Spirit of prophecy comes, everyone present will be able to prophesy or hear from God. This prophetic flow is so powerful and overwhelming that it can envelop whole nations. It is like a mighty river that cannot be quenched, stopped, or stayed from its course. The prophetic flow has such power that those present know "that God is in you of a truth" (1 Cor. 14:25).

God's Spirit is in the Church

Understanding and allowing the prophetic Spirit to flow in the church is vital to the life of the church. With it comes renewal, revival, restoration, and reformation. For us to receive these things, we need to know how to cultivate an atmosphere for the Spirit of prophecy to flow freely in the church. The ability to hear God creates an atmosphere for the Spirit of prophecy to flow in and through our lives.

Because of this, I want to take another look at what Moses said about hearing God speak to us individually. This is probably the clearest instruction in scripture about the way in which God speaks. Moses gives practical guidelines to learn how to listen to God. As such, this is one of the most important teachings in all of scriptures, for it reveals that it is the heartbeat of God to speak to us everyday.

Rediscovering the Prophetic Flow

Moses said, "...my speech shall distill as the dew, as the small rain upon the tender herb, and as the showers upon the grass" (Deut. 32:2). This is an awesome picture of God speaking to us, showing how, why, and when He speaks. It contains the clearest revelation of the ways He speaks to His people.

When we understand the ways of God in speaking to us, it will be easier for us to discern His voice in the midst of other voices that are competing for our attention. Hearing Him will become a joy as it is meant to be. We will learn what prophets and sages throughout the centuries have sought to teach—the way God speaks. Within this revelation will come a manifestation of God's will in our lives.

The will of God becomes clear to those who hear from Him. It opens to us the realm of possibility, for all things are possible with God. The voice of God will literally communicate faith into our lives so we can accomplish what God has called us to do (Rom. 10:17). We will be connected with God, for we will be tuned in to His voice. This divine connection will bring about an expression of His will and a demonstration of His kingdom in our lives. Praise God!

Tuning In to God

Since the days of Moses, God has been longing for people who would hear Him. He revealed His ways to Moses to share with the children of Israel so they could tune in to hear the voice of God. But a veil came over their eyes, preventing them from understanding what Moses said (2 Cor. 3:13). They were blinded to the fact that God wanted to intimately communicate with them, separately from the work of the priesthood. The same is true today.

Many believers today will go to a pastor or prophet to hear from God. They want someone else to hear God for them, just as the children of Israel did. They don't want to take the time necessary to cultivate a living relationship with Him. Instead, they would rather depend on someone else. Hearing from God becomes a once-a-week or once-a-year thing, rather than a daily experience. We have been fooled into accepting a counterfeit "Churchianity" rather than genuine Christianity.

Genuine Christianity is built upon listening to God. We need this as much as the grass needs the morning dew. Without that morning dew, the grass will dry out and burn up. Like the grass, we need the ever-present refreshing of God's voice every morning. We need His speech to "distill upon our lives like the dew upon the grass, as the small rain upon the tender herb" (Deut. 32:2).

The greatest need for believers is to wait upon God, allowing Him the necessary time to speak to us. For the most part, we are so stirred up doing things for God that we never take the time to be with Him. Jesus made it clear that one thing is needful—to spend time sitting at His feet, learning His ways and listening to His voice (Lk. 10:42). If we would do this, everything else would take care of itself, and we wouldn't waste our lives doing unprofitable things.

The Distilled Voice of God

Allowing the Holy Spirit to rest upon our lives allows us to become profitable, productive, fruitful believers. It means we have learned how to distinguish the voice of God from the other voices in our lives (1 Cor. 14:10). This is essential to being refreshed by the waters of God's Spirit. Because of this, it is important for us to learn how to discern or distill the voice of God.

How can we learn to distill the voice of God? This can be answered by looking at the morning dew, which is nothing more than condensation of water on grass. This condensation happens when bodies cool down at night. This cooling-down process enables the water in the air to condense and become dew. God's voice distills upon our lives in the same way. This means that we must go through a cooling-down process.

Cooling down is synonymous with slowing down.

Slowing down enables us to hear what God is saying. This means not allowing the busyness of life to drag us into a place of spiritual deafness. Spiritual deafness is a choice we make when we don't take time from our busy schedules to listen for Him. Listening means waiting and praying. This is the lost art of spiritual contemplation—waiting in the presence of God (Is. 40:31).

Making Time for God

When we wait in God's presence every day, He will speak to us every day. When we make hearing God a priority, He will make speaking to us a priority. This means we may have to make tradeoffs. We may not be able to watch as much television, to listen to our favorite radio shows, or to inundate our days off with so many distractions. We need to take time to hear from heaven if we want heaven to speak to us.

Jesus said it this way, "Where your treasure is, there will your heart be also" (Mt. 6:21). We can determine what we treasure by honestly looking at what we do. Then we will see who we really are. In this process of learning who we are by what we do, we will see what we truly value. And what we truly value will determine the quality of our spiritual lives. We cannot have great spiritual lives without spending quality time with God. It is that simple.

Notice what Moses says about the amount of

refreshing we receive through God's voice. He tells us that as we spend more time listening to God, we receive greater refreshing from His presence. This is revealed by Moses' description first of the dew, then the tender rain, and finally the showers. In other words, practicing God's presence releases His voice in ever greater, richer, deeper ways.

Increasing the Prophetic Flow

The refreshing waters that come through the God's voice can increase as we learn how to distill His voice from those around us. Because of this, the prophetic flow upon our lives can also increase, helping us grow in our ability to speak for God. This gift is not just for some—it is for all of us as we learn to "cool down" so we can hear God. This is the desire of His heart; He longs for people who love listening to Him.

Only this can release the spirit of prophecy into the church in greater measure. I believe it will bring about one of the greatest revivals the world has ever seen. God wants to soften our hearts to hear His voice so we can do what He says, which will release His power on the earth. God's power is released through the prophetic flow, bringing a visible manifestation of the Spirit of prophecy (Acts 1:8).

God is taking His church to this place, so we must get ready. It is time for the gospel to be more than just in word—we need to see God's unbridled power. This can happen only as we learn how to flow with the Holy Spirit, which precipitates the release of His power. We need this power. God wants us to have it, and we need to learn how to take hold of it. This is the subject of the next chapter.

Chapter Six

Flowing in the Holy Spirit

Something is missing in the church today. In spite of all of our programs, seminars, and conferences, we lack God's power. We really don't know very much about it. Even though we have heard about, desired, prayed for, and in some cases fasted for this power, we have yet to see it. Why is this? What is it that hinders us from sensing a tangible release of God's power into the church?

Rediscovering the Power of the Spirit

I love to read biographies of the great heroes of the faith who visibly demonstrated God's power. I have read about Smith Wigglesworth, A. A. Allen,

Kathryn Kulman, Jack Coe, John Lake, Alexander Dowie, Maria Woodworth-Etter, and others. As I have studied their lives, I have come to understand that they had a common theme: they all knew how to move with the person of the Holy Spirit (Gal. 3:5).

Many seminaries and Bible colleges do not teach about moving in the Holy Spirit. As such, few leaders within the church know how to flow with Him. It has taken me years to understand how and why He works the way He does (Gal. 5:16–19). And in spite of all I have learned, I am still just beginning to understand what God has called me to do.

I recently had a dream that illustrates what I am saying. I dreamed about a well-known prophet who was preparing to speak at a conference. Before he spoke, he was praying about a certain country. I also prayed very loudly about that country from my seat. When we both finished, he said that he felt something, and started sharing his message. As he was sharing, people started coming in very loudly with no regard for what he was saying. Children were running everywhere (by the way, I love children) and were definitely distracting this man of God. Then babies from outside the sanctuary started crying loudly. He walked over and shut the door to keep out the noise. A man sitting next to me asked what I thought about him. I said that he is different from most of today's prophets in that he knows how to flow in the Holy Ghost.

Getting Plugged into the Power

This dream illustrates that what is often spoken today in the Lord's name is from the gifting of the prophet rather than the flow of the Holy Spirit. I do not think it is wrong to flow in the prophetic gift. I think this is good. Yet there is something better that few prophets today understand, which is how to flow in the Holy Spirit. This is like plugging the gifts of God into the power socket of the Spirit.

Plugging into God's power means learning how to flow in the Holy Spirit. This is different from being led by or even walking in the Spirit. Flowing in the Holy Spirit means to allow Him to carry us wherever He wants us to go (2 Pet. 1:21). This is how prophets in Old Testament spoke the prophetic word. They had unction to function in the prophetic. Their words flowed out of their connection to the Holy Spirit, which is why their words were confirmed by such dramatic events (Is. 38:8). God confirmed the word of His servants as well as the word of His Spirit. This is an awesome reality and has the potential to release God's power into our midst.

Maturing in Prophecy and Power

The power of God flows when the Holy Spirit is present. He longs to move in power in our midst (Rom. 8:26). He is looking for individuals who are willing to bend their will to His. Evan Roberts and

Kathryn Kulman were such awesome releasers of God's power because they knew how to plug into the Holy Spirit. It was this ability that moved countless masses into the kingdom. This is what we need in our day.

Yet for us to have this, we must learn from those who have gone before us. We must study the lives of those who knew how to flow in the Holy Spirit so that we can learn by imitation to do the same. Today we need men and women who know how to flow in the Holy Spirit and release His power to hurting humanity. It isn't enough to merely hear the stories, but they must propel us into a new dimension of experience.

This is especially true for those who are called into prophetic ministry. We should minister in prophecy to congregations only to the degree that we have learned how to flow with the Holy Spirit. Why? Because then the entire body will be blessed by the words we give rather than us simply feeling relieved that we have spoken from our hearts. Discerning the difference is an important step in the maturity of prophetic ministry.

Amplifying the Gift

The prophetic flow is following what the Holy Spirit is saying in prophecy. This means we have laid down our agenda and have tuned in to His. The Holy

Spirit's agenda for every meeting is to glorify Jesus. This may be done through prophecy or through other signs of His presence such as miracles, healing, joy, faith, and so on.

When the Holy Spirit decides to move in a service, He may release a Spirit of prophecy. As this Spirit is released, everyone present will be able to speak prophetically, although not everyone should (1 Cor. 14:12). This release of the Spirit of prophecy into a church can have a dramatic impact upon those present. It will cause them to open their spirits to hear from God. Spiritual deafness and blindness in the church are driven out through the Spirit of prophecy.

The Spirit of prophecy is actually an amplification of the gift of prophecy in the church (Phil. 1:20). As such, more prophecy is released when the Spirit of prophecy is in operation. This amplification comes when a mature person in the office of prophet flows in the Holy Spirit, thereby releasing the Spirit of prophecy into the service. This release of the Spirit of prophecy can potentially cause all present to move in it.

This flow can be so strong that everyone present will prophesy, even those who are not necessarily used in prophecy. An example of this in scripture is Saul, who prophesied when he came into the midst of prophets. This must have been an astonishing transformation because those who heard him said, "Is Saul also among the prophets?" (1 Sam. 10:11.) They thought he was one of the sons of the prophets because of the Spirit of prophecy that came upon him.

The First Seminaries: Schools for Prophecy

Who were the sons of the prophets, and why was the Spirit of prophecy upon them so mightily? They were actually schools where senior prophets would train others in how to move in prophecy. Often a senior prophet would have one or more schools, as did Samuel, Elijah, and Elisha. All of the budding prophets under their care recognized their authority as leaders.

Being a senior prophet was more than just in word—it was in power and demonstration. They were identified by the signs and wonders that followed them. When they spoke, God confirmed their words with supernatural signs in heaven and earth. This awesome demonstration of God's power kept the budding prophets honest, for they knew that God's Spirit rested upon the senior prophet (2 Kgs. 5:26).

Because of their special relationship with the senior prophets, often the budding prophets were called sons of the prophets. This is how these schools came to be recognized by this term. Often the senior prophets would take on the role of being spiritual fathers to the budding prophets. This is why Elisha called Elijah his father—he recognized the authority God had placed upon Elijah for his own well-being and protection (2 Kgs. 2:12).

These were the first seminaries in scripture. God used these schools to train people with a prophetic calling to hear, speak, and move in the Spirit of prophecy. This was an awesome honor and carried with it a great deal of respect. Being associated with a school of prophets was like going to Harvard, Yale, or Princeton. It was the finest education available. This is where almost all of the Biblical prophets were trained to speak the word of God.

Restoring the Prophetic Community

This cuts against the grain of our perception of Israel's prophets. We imagine them being wild-eyed fanatics with little earthly relevance who loved to minister words of judgment. This was captured recently in a major Christian magazine, with a picture of a prophet dressed like Moses or John the Baptist pointing his finger at a group of fearful church members. The accompanying article was about the importance of prophetic etiquette in the church.

I agree that the church needs prophetic etiquette, but we also need to understand the true nature of prophecy. How can we think of someone who always points his finger as being a true prophet when the

Scripture so clearly calls this practice sin? (Is. 58:9.) We need a radical shift in our perception of what prophets are and how they are called, trained, matured, and released into ministry. This will change the face of prophetic ministry in the church.

I believe that for the perception of prophetic ministry to change within the church, schools of prophecy must be established. This is happening in many places around the world today. I know many senior prophets who are rising up and training believers called into prophetic ministry. This is exciting, for it reveals exciting changes happening in how we view the church, especially the importance of prophecy.

Several prophets' schools are being raised up of which I am personally aware. One is being established in England by Graham Cooke. Another is starting in Kansas City by Mike Bickle and Paul Cain. Others are being launched by Bill Hamon and Leon Walters in Florida and Indiana. Still others are being initiated by Jonathan David, John Paul Jackson, and Rick Joyner. Many more could be mentioned from around the world. Praise God for the release of the Spirit of prophecy!

Reaching for the Fullness of Christ in Prophecy

These schools will become increasingly important in the days ahead in bringing the prophetic ministry and office to their fullness. The church desperately needs what these schools have to offer, and they are essential to the purposes of God. We need what each schools offers, for each one brings a different flavor of the prophetic flow to us. These flavors emphasize certain parts of the prophetic ministry.

In the Old Testament, each prophet school had a certain calling it was responsible to bring forth. This can be seen by the names and examples of the prophet schools in Israel (2 Kgs. 2:1–7). The five main prophet schools in Israel were located in Bethel, Gilgal, Jericho, Mizpeh and Ramah (although I personally believe that there were more than five schools). Each one of these prophet schools had a special calling or impartation that it made upon its students.

This is a powerful teaching, for it reveals the depths and dimensions of the prophetic calling. I will save this for a later book on the office and ministry of the prophet entitled *Entering the School of the Prophets*. Suffice it to say that the prophet schools were extremely important to the purposes of God—He used them to bring His liberating word to the people who needed to enter into His will. The same will be true today as we allow God to raise His prophets and prophetic people into the fullness of their calling.

As prophets and prophetic people are released into the fullness of their calling, they will enable us to tune in to what the Holy Spirit is saying and doing in the church today. This is vital for us to become all that God wants us to be. We cannot become who we were designed to be, or do what we are called to do, without the unction from the Holy Spirit. We need God to breathe life into us through the Spirit of prophecy in our midst. This can happen only as we hear and respond to what God is saying.

Knowing the Word, Will, and Ways of God

Some of the greatest hindrances to Holy Spirit moving in our midst are those who are ignorant of Him and His ways. Knowing the word of God and knowing God are two different things. We can know God's word and still be ignorant of His person or power (Mt. 22:29). This is a reason why so many who claim to know the word of God are mired in hypocrisy. They have never learned about God beyond His word. So we need to experience God in fresh new ways every day by the Spirit of prophecy.

Think about it: the Pharisees knew and surrounded themselves with God's word, but when the Word of God in the person of Christ showed up, they didn't recognize him (John 5:39,40). The same thing can happen to us if we don't allow the Spirit of the word to saturate us everyday. We need to surrender our wills to the word of God and the Spirit of God so we can flow in the Spirit of prophecy.

Flowing in the Spirit of prophecy starts with learning the word of God. We need His word to anchor us to His will so we don't get lost in the depths of His Spirit (Heb. 6:19). The word of God is a map that gives us an overall perspective of where we are going. It helps us chart a course that safely brings us to the revealed will of God for our lives. This is why we need to understand God's word.

Once we understand the word of God and start living our lives according to its principles, we will become more sensitive to spiritual things (Heb. 5:12–14). Then we can begin walking in the Holy Spirit and will become keenly aware of His presence. This will enable us to hear Him guiding us into deeper spiritual realms. We will live, walk, and even be carried by the Spirit.

Everyone Can Get in the Flow

God desires this for every believer. We are all to have this kind of intimacy with Him. This is not reserved for mystics or super-spiritual believers, but it is for everyday people. Each one of us has been designed by God to live, walk, and move in the Holy Spirit (Gal. 5:16,18,25). This means that all of us can flow in the Spirit of prophecy. We can all live in it, speaking to others as God wills. This is true whether we ourselves are gifted prophetically or not.

I can say this because the church itself is prophetic. All of us have access to the Spirit of prophecy that is designed to flow in the church. Because of this, every believer may prophesy. Even the testimonies that we give are forms of prophecy. The testimony of Jesus in our lives is the Spirit of prophecy at work in us (Rev. 19:10). God is literally speaking through our lives whether we realize it or not.

This can be quite a shock for most believers. We go about our daily tasks, but often don't realize how much God is intimately involved in the actions we take. The Bible says that our steps are "ordered by the Lord" (Ps. 37:23). God is drawing us into a way that is good for us. No wonder the Word of God says, "It is God which worketh in you both to will and to do of His good pleasure" (Phil. 2:13). And again, "He is able to do exceeding abundantly above all that we ask or think" (Eph. 3:20).

You are Part of the Team

Our God is awesome. He knows how to direct our work in truth (Is. 61:8). He also knows how to bring us where we should be, even when we don't know where we are going. Our path is being set, and God is the one who is orchestrating our steps. This is the sovereignty of our Savior. Jesus really is in full control of our lives and the universe around us (Heb. 1:3). Everything has been planned from the foundation of the world (Heb. 4:3). As such, many of the things in our lives are prophetic.

Have you thought about this truth? You are part of a prophetic drama that is unfolding on the earth. God is the author of this drama. A villain named Satan is intent on destroying your part in this great drama. He doesn't want you to fulfill the purpose for which you are created. If he can keep you from playing your part, everyone suffers and this hinders the flow of prophecy through the church.

God has given each of us an important part to play. Anything we do or don't do can have a tremendous impact on the final production of this great end-time drama. In this epic prophetic drama, every person is vital, even the seemingly most insignificant member. This is why Paul, the great apostle of the faith, said, "…those members of the body, which seem to be more feeble, are necessary…" (1 Cor. 12:22). What an awesome way to view the body of Christ.

We need to truly see the church through this kind of prophetic vision. I long for the day when the church comes to this place where we see neither black nor white, male nor female, rich nor poor, clergy nor layperson, but Christ is all and in all (Gal. 3:28, Col. 3:11). The prophetic flow is all about bringing us to a place where Christ is glorified. Only then will Christ be the one we see, and His vision for us will be fulfilled. We will have a vision of who He is, who we are, and who we can be in Him. May God bring us to this point.

A Final Word

God is moving in our day to release the Spirit of prophecy into the Church. We need it in our midst as well as a Spirit of holiness. God is cleaning up His church so we can move into the Spirit of prophecy by the Spirit of holiness, lest His judgments rest upon His church. This is why such a tremendous conviction of sin is in the church today.

God has released the Spirit of conviction to bring His people to repentance. For many, this is very uncomfortable. We are not used to the Spirit of God falling on us to convict us of sin. In fact, some of us are not even sure it is the Holy Spirit who is convicting us of our guilt to bring change in our lives.

As a result, some have fallen deeper and deeper into sin. We have not given heed to our consciences or to the conviction of the Holy Spirit in our midst. If we continue down this path, God will remove His Spirit and lampstand from us. This would not be good for the church or nation of America, for we are here to bring light to those around us.

My hope is that we will submit to God's Spirit of conviction so He can bring His Spirit of prophecy into the church in a greater way. This generation is longing to see a genuine display of the supernatural power of God. They want us to speak of the things that only God can know. They want us to show them what our God can do.

As the old saying goes, talk is cheap, and actions speak louder than words. What do our actions tell the world about what we believe? Are we genuinely pointing them to Jesus Christ through our deeds? Anyone can minister to people in the natural. Many good people do this, and we need more of them in our day. Yet our good deeds can never replace God's deeds that people long to see.

We are surrounded by people in need of a God who will touch them where they hurt. We can be a part of the answer as we plug into the Spirit of prophecy. As Jesus said, "Ye are the light of the world. A city that is set on a hill cannot be hid. Let your light so shine before men, that they may see your good works, and glorify your Father which is in heaven" (Mt. 5:14,16). Get ready to shine!

Printed in the United States
71533LV00002B/232